RESEARCHING ANTHROPOLOGY ON THE INTERNET

Second Edition

David L. Carlson
Texas A&M University

THOMSON

WADSWORTH

Australia • Canada • Mexico • Singapore • Spain • United Kingdom • United States

For more information about our
products, contact us at:
Thomson Learning Academic
Resource Center
1-800-423-0563

For permission to use material from
this text, contact us by:
Phone: 1-800-730-2214
Fax: 1-800-731-2215
Web: www.thomsonrights.com

Asia
Thomson Learning
5 Shenton Way #01-01
UIC Building
Singapore 068808

Australia
Nelson Thomson Learning
102 Dodds Street
South Street
South Melbourne, Victoria 3205
Australia

Canada
Nelson Thomson Learning
1120 Birchmount Road
Toronto, Ontario M1K 5G4
Canada

Europe/Middle East/South Africa
Thomson Learning
High Holborn House
50-51 Bedford Row
London WC1R 4LR
United Kingdom

Latin America
Thomson Learning
Seneca, 53
Colonia Polanco
11560 Mexico D.F.
Mexico

Spain
Paraninfo Thomson Learning
Calle/Magallanes, 25
28015 Madrid, Spain

Table of Contents

Preface vi

Part I. Guide to Using the Internet 1
    Introduction 1
    Frequently Asked Questions 2
    Communicating 19
    Simple Searches 29
    Research on the Web 34
    Current Events 38
    Learning 40

Part II. Researching Anthropology on the Web 42
    Introduction 42
    Cultural Anthropology 43
    Physical Anthropology 54
    Archaeology 60
    Applied Anthropology 70
    Applying Anthropology 81
    Careers in Anthropology 87
    Conclusion 93

Glossary 94

Preface

This guide is written for students who are generally familiar with the World Wide Web and the Internet, but do not have much experience using the web to study anthropology. Part I of the guide provides you with the answers to some simple questions about the Internet and the World Wide Web. Basic tasks such as communicating, searching, and learning are covered in some detail with a focus on how to use the Internet to place the study of anthropology into a broader context. Addresses for the web sites mentioned in the text are included at the end of each section. Part II focuses in more detail on parts of the World Wide Web that cover anthropology. Cultural anthropology (including linguistics), physical anthropology, archaeology, and applied anthropology are all discussed. Within each of these fields, specific web sites that are good starting points are identified. In addition, there are sections on applying anthropology (as a volunteer, field school participant, or intern) and how to find a job in anthropology.

If you are a student, this guide can help you to prepare for class and complete course assignments. The Internet is not a replacement for using the resources in your school library, but it can help you to find those resources more effectively. It can also help you find material that is not locally available. You can use the Internet to keep up to date on current news reports that cover areas of the world or topics that are covered in your textbook or in class lectures. That information can help you to be a better student in several ways. You will be able to ask better questions in class and you will remember things better if you link what you are learning in the classroom to what is going on in the world around you. You will also develop better skills as a critical thinker, because you will find many competing viewpoints on the web. Evaluating these sites will strengthen your ability to evaluate arguments and compare contrasting views.

If you are an anthropology instructor, you may be looking for ways to incorporate this guide into your course. There are at least eight ways you can use the information in this guide to create classroom assignments.

1. Read a specific document on the web and answer questions. This is a good way for students to begin to become comfortable with the web.

2. Read a specific document on the web and evaluate its credibility. This activity asks students to apply critical judgement to the materials they find on the web. It requires little of the student in the way of web-expertise, but helps them develop their evaluation skills.

3. Find specific data on the web. This activity is slightly more challenging since students must use search engines to locate the answers and may have to evaluate the quality of alternate sources. In some cases there may be more than one "correct" answer so that evaluation of this activity should focus on the process of locating and evaluating the information more than the specific answer.

4. Find a specific kind of site on the web. Ask students to find one or more web sites that are designed for a specific audience. There is no "correct answer" but students learn how to find sites on the web and get the flexibility of seeking sites that relate to their individual interests.

5. Research an issue on the web. Here the question is broader and the issue involves strong proponents for opposite positions. This activity involves more skill in searching the web for information and in sifting through numerous possible web sites for those that are relevant to the topic. It also involves a critical evaluation of two or more positions.

6. Several companies who produce documentaries routinely create web sites to complement the programs they broadcast on air. You can assign students to use the material on the web site to lead a class discussion about the documentary after they have viewed it.

7. Require students to use some resources from the web in their research papers. The web should not be the only source of information, but requiring students to search for information on a specific topic will help them develop their search skills and learn how to evaluate and cite material they find on the web.

8. Studying the culture of the net. Here the web is not a resource for information; it is an example of virtual culture for the student to investigate. These activities do not focus on facts or competing positions, but instead on how the web creates new opportunities for cultural interaction and how the web contributes to the development of a global culture.

These are just some starting points for incorporating the Internet into your anthropology classes. As you and your students become more familiar with the web, you will certainly find other interesting ways to integrate the web into your classes. As you do, I would very much like to hear about them.

David L. Carlson
Texas A&M University
dcarlson@tamu.edu

PART I.
GUIDE TO USING THE INTERNET

Introduction

You probably already use the Internet. It is mentioned on the news and in newspapers and magazines every day. It is either the greatest boon to modern civilization or the greatest curse. As a student of anthropology, you probably have an opinion on this debate. This guide does not attempt to resolve that issue, but it does provide you with basic information concerning what is available on the Internet and how you find it. Once you know how to locate information, you will be able to find out more about any of the topics discussed here. If you know little about the Internet, this guide is your first step. If you are already an experienced net surfer, this guide may give you some new ideas about how to use the web to enhance your education. The Internet does not render traditional methods of communication and education obsolete; instead it supplements and amplifies them. In order to use the net you will need to develop new skills and refine ones that you already have.

The **Internet** (or just "net") is a "network of networks." It is a standard method by which computers can communicate with one another regardless of whether they are large or small computers and regardless of the operating system they use. It is a kind of universal language for computers. At first the primary use of the net was for electronic mail, transferring files, and operating computers remotely. More recently, additional functions have been added to make it easier to exchange information and ideas over the net. The most important of these is a way of transferring pages of information containing text, multimedia, and links to other pages. These **hypertext** pages are re-trieved and displayed by programs called **"browsers."** Collectively, these pages make up the part of the Internet called the **"World Wide Web"** (or just "web"). Although the **Net** refers to the interconnected networks and the **Web** refers to the interlinked hypertext pages, most people do not distinguish between the two consistently. In this guide I will use the terms interchangeably.

A reasonable way of visualizing the Internet is to think of a series of nodes (computers or whole computer networks) that are connected to one another. Each node is connected to only a few other nodes so getting information from one node to another one means that the infor-mation travels through many other nodes before reaching its destination. This roundabout approach makes it simpler to add a new node since

1

only a few connections need to be added and it also means that information has many different paths that it could take in getting from one node to another. If one path is broken, the information is just rerouted along another set of paths. The network does not care what kind of information is being moved. It could be an email file, a picture, a sound file, or a video.

The guide is divided into two sections. The first part answers "Frequently Asked Questions" (**FAQs**) about the Internet and the World Wide Web and describes how you can use the net as a student. The addresses of the web sites (the Universal Resource Locators or **URLs**) are listed at the end of each section. The second part of the guide focuses specifically on how to use the net to enhance your understanding of anthropology and provides useful information for researching specific topics within the fields of cultural anthropology, physical anthropology, archaeology, applied anthropology, volunteer opportunities in anthropology, and careers in anthropology

Frequently Asked Questions

Where did the Internet come from? The history of the Internet and the World Wide Web is interesting because it developed from a few simple requirements for a robust network. It grew amazingly fast into a global information network linking millions of people and millions of pages together.

What do I need to get on the Net? This short section gives you some pointers to getting started on the web. Since there are differences in computers, software, and methods of connecting to the Net, it may not meet your exact needs, but it should help you to ask knowledgeable questions.

What kinds of information will I find on the Web? This section talks about the different kinds of files on the Web. Some can be viewed directly with your browser software (probably Netscape or Internet Explorer), but others require special programs. The file types and the special programs you may need are summarized here.

Is it safe? News media enjoy running stories on the dangers of the Net. This section provides a brief introduction to potential hazards on the Net including viruses, cookies, java programs, and communicating with strangers.

Is the information on the Net reliable? The simple answer is, "Some of it." This chapter gives you some basic tools to help you develop critical skills. Just as you cannot believe everything people tell you and you cannot believe everything you read in the paper, you cannot believe everything you read or see on the Web.

Where should I start? When you connect to the Net and start your browser, a start page is loaded. This section talks about start pages and **portals.** If you just want to explore the Web, you might try one of the Web Rings that links sites related to anthropology or the Virtual Library of Anthropology.

Where Did the Internet Come From?

The Internet was born thirty years ago in the midst of the Cold War. With the increasing threat of nuclear destruction, the U.S. military wanted to be able to operate computers remotely and wanted to be able to communicate over its computer network even if large parts of it were destroyed. This meant that the network had to be decentralized and it had to be possible to route information dynamically. Out of these requirements ARPANET began in 1969 with four nodes. It grew slowly at first. Nodes were added and at each node additional computers (hosts) were connected. By 1984 there were 1,000 hosts, by 1989 there were 100,000 and by 1992 there were 1,000,000. Today there are about 72 million hosts.

One of the important reasons for connecting computers was to allow people to access them remotely. Powerful computers were expensive and it was easier and less expensive to let researchers run programs on those computers remotely. Communication between people at the various nodes to ask for assistance or schedule time on a computer took the form of electronic messages (which were much cheaper than phone calls). As the net grew and the cost of computers dropped, the ability to run programs remotely became less important than the ability to send and receive electronic messages. **Email** quickly became one of the principal uses of the developing networks. As useful as electronic messages are, they are not very flexible if you want to circulate information among a group of people and allow them to discuss a topic. Two approaches to this problem were developed that expanded on the basic idea of email. The first was the **mailing list**, a computer program that would forward the same message to a list of addresses. If you subscribed to the list, you would receive any message that was sent to the list. The lists were not limited to serious topics. One of the first ones was SF-LOVERS for fans of science fiction. The second innovation was **electronic bulletin boards**. You sent your email message to the bulletin board where it remained for a period of time. Anyone who saw it could reply to you directly or could post their own message. The first bulletin

3

board system was USENET which began operating in 1979. There are separate bulletin boards (called newsgroups) for different topics. True to the decentralized concept of the Internet the USENET bulletin boards are located on many different computers which communicate with one another to keep their copies of the messages up to date.

Electronic mail and bulletin boards have proven valuable and have spread beyond the Internet. Bulletin board systems based on home computers with modems offered email to local subscribers and in 1983 many of these were linked together into a loose network called FidoNet. FidoNet was based entirely on communication over phone lines. Commercial information systems such as Compuserve, America Online and Prodigy also offered email. Within the last few years, virtually all of them have connected to the Internet so that the number of different (and incompatible) email systems is shrinking.

As the net grew, ways of using it expanded as well. One advantage that centralized commercial systems such as America Online had was the ability to allow people to communicate in real time by typing messages that were instantly distributed to others who were logged in. They could also play interactive games against one another in real time. A simple messaging system for sending a message to a single location was present in early versions of the Internet, but allowing several people to send messages at the same time was not really possible until the development of **Internet Relay Chat** in 1988.

Much of the software for the net was developed by people in their spare time and was made freely available for use by anyone else. The problem on the Internet was that you could only get a file if you knew exactly where it was. In 1990 a program called **Archie** was released that allowed people to search archives of hundreds of computers to find a particular program file.

The watershed year for the Internet as we know it today was 1991. A strong method of encrypting information was released (Pretty Good Privacy) which is closely related to the methods used today to encrypt commercial transactions. Encryption scrambles the text of the message so that, even if it is intercepted, it cannot be read. A new way of distributing textual information was introduced by researchers at the University of Minnesota called **Gopher**. Gopher exploded on the net as people began to make various kinds of information available. Since it distributed text only, it was well-suited to slow computers and slow Internet connections. Not so well suited at the time was a more complex system that allowed text and graphics files to be distributed and combined into a single page. Developed in Switzerland, it involved a way of formatting a document to contain text, graphics, and most importantly links to other documents. The links could be to documents or images located anywhere on the Internet. Because of this feature, the system was called the World-Wide Web (WWW). The only problem was that many people in 1991 still accessed the Internet via terminals that could not display graphics. Gopher grew rapidly for several years because it was designed around the limitations of existing equipment.

In 1992, the number of hosts on the Internet reached 1,000,000. The following year a graphical browser for the Internet was developed at the University of Illinois called **Mosaic**. The web caught up with and surpassed Gopher in that year. Universities and government agencies moved rapidly to the web. The US White House and the United Nations come online with the US Senate and House following in 1994. That same year the first shopping malls and cyberbanks begin to appear and Pizza Hut sold its first online pizza. To advertise their green card lottery services an Arizona law firm sent an email advertisements to thousands of people thereby introducing **"spam"** (the email equivalent of junk mail) to the net.

Since 1994, the number of web sites has grown dramatically. Several of the people who developed the Mosaic web browser left the University of Illinois to found Netscape, while Microsoft started shipping a web browser with its Windows 95 operating system. Competition between Microsoft and Netscape resulted in browsers absorbing the functions of many separate programs (for example email and news-readers). Limitations in the original web standards were removed by adding capabilities for multimedia (streaming audio and video, virtual reality modeling) and interactivity (Java and Shockwave programming). Although the capacity of the net has increased steadily, the growth in the number of users and the **bandwidth** (number of bits moved per second) for each user has grown at least as fast.

The Internet is big, but because it is decentralized, we can only make educated guesses about how big. The number of hosts on the net was nearly 150 million by early 2002. Estimates of how many people are online around the world vary from about 500 to 600 million. There are about 8 million web sites around the world.

What Do I Need to Get on the Net?

You will need four things to begin using the net: a computer (or access to one at your university computer center), a connection to a network, a browser, and a computer account (for email).

You can access the net with almost any **computer** made today. The net is accessible via IBM/Microsoft machines, Apple MacIntosh computers, unix workstations, and large mainframe systems. If you have your own computer, you are set. If you are a student at a university, there are probably computer labs where you can use a computer. Increasingly public libraries are also providing access to the net, so you might be able to access the net there.

Secondly, you need a **connection** to a network that is connected to the net. There are several kinds of connections and new options are being added. Many computers come with a modem that allows them to access a network over a telephone line. Modem connections have the advantage that you can use them to connect to the net wherever there is a phone jack. They have the disadvantage that they are the slowest way to connect. Your university probably provides much faster ethernet connections in computer labs, offices, some classrooms, and even dormitories. Ethernet connections are significantly faster and do not use your telephone line. Other options such as cable modems, satellite systems, and digital subscriber lines are available in parts of the country.

Thirdly, you may need a **browser**. A browser is a software application that allows you to retrieve and display web pages. Most computers come with them already installed. The two dominant programs are Netscape[1] and Internet Explorer[2] by Microsoft. Both browsers have the ability to access email and news groups, although there are dedicated programs for those functions as well that you may find more useful. When you start the browser, it will look much like a word processing program. You will see formatted text and graphics and you will be able to scroll up and down the page. The thing to remember is that the documents you view in the browser are not on your computer but somewhere else. On most web pages, underlined text identifies links to other documents. If you click your mouse on some underlined text, your browser will load the page defined by the link. Web pages use a cryptic addressing system called a **universal resource locator** (**URL**) that specifies a particular domain address and a particular file at that domain. Because the addresses are cumbersome to type (and the browser is very picky about spelling), you should **bookmark** pages you want to return to (check your browser's help files for instructions on how to bookmark a site).

You may discover that you need some additional programs to view some pages. These programs are referred to as **plug-ins** because they work within your browser. For example the Adobe Acrobat® plug-in allows you to view pages that have been specially formatted. Several plug-ins give you the ability to play video and sound files while others

allow you to maneuver within a three dimensional virtual space (VRML).
Any of these programs can be downloaded once you are on the net.

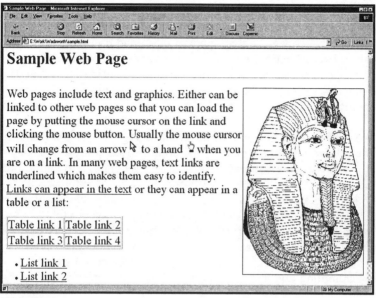

Web Browser

Sites that have content requiring these programs usually provide a link
that you can use to download and install the software.

Finally, you need a computer **account**. Your university computer
center probably has information about how to get a student account.
You can also get an account with an Internet Service Provider (ISP). The
account allows you to log on to the network and provides storage space
for email messages that people send you until you retrieve or discard
them. Internet providers include national firms such as America Online
and AT&T as well as local firms that serve a single region.

What Types of Media Are on the Web?

As originally conceived, web documents consisted of formatted text
and images. Soon other kinds of media were added to web pages. First
sound and pre-formatted documents, then animations and virtual spaces,
and finally video were added. Unfortunately web browsers could not
handle these content types directly so **plug-in** programs that could
handle the new content types either within the browser window or in a
separate window were developed. As new content types were intro-

7

duced, so too were new formats requiring more than one plug-in program for each content type. A new series of plug-ins tries to deal with multiple content types in an effort to reduce the confusion somewhat. Currently on the web you will find all of the following types of media:

HTML Text. These are the standard files used on web sites. They are formatted using "Hyper-Text Markup Language" (HTML) which means that the file contains text and codes (markup language) to tell your web browser how to format the text and where to set up links to other documents.

Pre-Formatted Text. In contrast to html documents, pre-formatted documents are not interpreted by the web browser, but are displayed exactly as they are presented without markup codes. In general, browsers will not try to format documents that have a file extension of "txt" which is the most common way of identifying ASCII documents. These documents are displayed in your browser using a fixed pitch font (such as Courier) whereas HTML documents are generally displayed using a variable pitch font (such as Times Roman). ASCII is mostly used for older files that have not been converted to HTML and for programs (where indenting and line breaks help to make the program more legible).

HTML documents do not give you complete control over how your document will look on someone else's computer. HTML does not support some common formatting features (notably tabs). Browsers do not always wrap text around images in the same way and the sizing of table rows and columns can differ for different browsers and for different versions of a particular browser. For these reasons you will find some documents on the web that are not written in HTML. These pre-formatted documents use other ways of composing a document. Currently the most common alternate format is Adobe® Acrobat. Acrobat allows you to take a document from a word processing, spreadsheet, or presentation program and preserve all of the original formatting. The only drawback is that the new file cannot be interpreted directly by your browser. Adobe provides Acrobat Reader[3], a free program that can read Acrobat files. The reader will display the Acrobat file in the browser window.

Images. Image files come in several varieties and most web browsers support them without needing any plug-in programs. The most common types on the web include GIF, JPG, and TIFF. Each has some differences that make them more appropriate in certain circumstances. GIF and TIFF files preserve every pixel in the original file (so they are referred to as "lossless"). In most cases they will require larger files than JPG, which preserves most of the information (so they are referred to as "lossy"). Typically you will not notice the difference between the two,

8

except that the JPG image will load much faster. TIFF files are usually used to provide high-resolution images that can be used by news media or for presentations.

Sound. There are many types of audio files on the web. Standard audio files contain a digital encoding of sound. They can be very large, on the order of 20K to 60K per second. For that reason these formats are usually used to record short theme songs, snappy quotations, and sound effects. You will run across three types on the web, each associated with a different computer type: AU (UNIX), AIFF (Macintosh), and WAV (Windows). Increasingly, the web seems to be standardizing on WAV files.

MIDI files store the instructions for creating a melody or tune. MIDI files are much smaller, but require a sound card in your computer that uses the instructions to create the sounds, much like a player piano plays songs by following coded instructions on a role of paper. The drawback of MIDI files is that they will sound somewhat different depending on the software and hardware that is used to play them.

Recently, a method has been developed of compressing sound files by discarding some of the details so that the files are smaller and the download times are shorter. These compressed audio files are called MP3 and are used extensively to record music. There are whole web sites devoted to programs that are used to play these files and to listings of music that have been encoded.

The sound files just mentioned all have to be downloaded to your computer's hard drive before they can be played. This means that they cannot be used for live sound such as that of a radio broadcast. Streaming audio files, in contrast, begin playing as soon as part of the file has arrived. This feature makes it possible to send live broadcasts over the web, and allows you to listen to longer programs. The two dominant formats for streaming audio are RealAudio and Windows Media Audio (wma). Microsoft's Windows Media Player[4] and Real Network's RealOne Player[5] can play these files.

Virtual Spaces. Virtual spaces create a world that you can explore by using a set of controls on the bottom and sides of your browser window. You can view the world from any angle, up close or far away. They are still in the formative stages. They usually involve large files and your movement through the world may not be smooth unless the world is simple and your computer has lots of memory and a fast processor. You will need a plug-in program to experience virtual spaces and there are several for each of the major browsers. A number of virtual worlds that recreate archaeological sites and great architectural structures are available on the web.

Video. As with sound, the first file formats for video compress the images into a single, very large file. There are three major formats: MOV (Apple QuickTime[6]), AVI (Microsoft Audio Visual), and MPEG. The biggest drawback to these formats is that you have to wait for the entire file to download so live broadcasts are not feasible and the amount of video you can download is limited by your available hard disk space.

Streaming video works like streaming audio. You begin watching the video while it is downloading. The entire file is not stored on your computer, so you are not limited by your available hard disk space. The major plug-ins for viewing video are RealOne Player by Real Networks and the Windows Media Player by Microsoft.

Program Files. These are binary files containing machine language instructions designed to work on your computer. Web browsers will usually ask if you want to run the program directly or save it on your hard drive. Usually you will save the program and then run it to install the program. Download these programs only from reliable sources to avoid the possibility of getting one that contains a virus.

Is It Safe?

As long as you take sensible precautions, the net is safe. Growing up in contemporary society, we are accustomed to interacting with strangers in public settings. Since we access the net from the privacy of our homes or offices, it is easy to forget that the net is a public place. Information on the net does not travel directly from your computer to the computer you are contacting. It travels a circuitous route through many other computers. Each step along the route involves making a copy of your information, sending it to the next computer along the way, and then deleting the copy. Unless the information is encrypted, it can be viewed by someone else. Online vendors now generally encrypt all sensitive information (such as name, address, credit card number) and web browsers use an icon (usually some kind of padlock) to let you know that the information is being encrypted. On the other hand, it is rare for email messages to be encrypted. Unless you are encrypting your message, don't include information that you don't want others to see.

Another security concern involves information that you provide to a company or vendor when you register at their web site, which means providing your name, email address, and possibly other information. Usually registration involves storing some information on your computer (a file called a cookie). Web pages use cookies to recognize when you return to their site. This allows them to customize their pages according to your interests (and to try to pick advertising that you would be more likely to find interesting). Cookie files are also needed when you customize a web page (for example, you set up a special version of Yahoo! called My Yahoo!). When you are at a shopping site, cookies are used to keep track of your selections until you complete your purchase. You can set your browser to notify you when a web page tries to store information on your computer, and you can set your browser to refuse all cookie files.

Your name and email address are probably already available on the web unless you have had your account for a short time. Your university may include some information about you in a publicly accessible directory unless you specifically request that they not do so. You should be very careful with your social security number or credit card numbers. Before providing any information, make sure that the web site indicates how it will use the information. There are currently no U.S. laws protecting your privacy when you provide information to a web site. Legislation may be proposed in the future and the European Union has put strong restrictions in place that may eventually become a model for the U.S.

A third area of concern involves computer viruses and other attacks on your computer as a result of your connection to the net. Again, taking reasonable precautions will protect you or will minimize the damage if your computer is infected. The most important precaution (and the one you are most likely to ignore) is to keep up-to-date backup copies of important files on your computers. You do not need to backup software programs since you have the original distribution disks, but you should backup text, graphics, and spreadsheet files that you have created. Computers are very reliable, but they all fail eventually. If you lose valuable information or work, it will be no consolation to know that it was caused by a hard disk crash rather than a virus.

A computer virus is a small program that copies itself to the hard disk on your computer (and often to any floppy disk inserted in the computer). It typically hides itself by attaching to programs already present on your hard drive, particularly the system files that load whenever you turn your computer on. Some viruses simply put silly messages on your screen, others slow your computer down, and others deliberately damage or erase files. Software that detects viruses is readily available and should help you to avoid infection. Since a virus is a program, you generally cannot be infected from a text, graphic, or spreadsheet file. As computer software has become more complex, it has become possible to embed macro commands (small simple programs) into these files. Software manufacturers have taken steps to prevent these macro commands from being used to insert viruses, but no one can guarantee the continued effectiveness of these measures.

Your computer can be a target for hackers if you are linked through an ethernet connection or a cable modem and you leave your computer turned on. Make certain that you have set the security features in your operating system to restrict access to your disk drives. If you want others to be able to access files on your computer (such as your web pages), put them in a subdirectory and restrict access to that subdirectory.

You will meet people on the net via email, electronic conferences, chat rooms, via web pages, or through personal ads that people place on the net (just like those found in newspapers). Remember that you do not have many of the cues that you subconsciously use to size people up. They control every statement that they make to you ("slips of the tongue" are much less likely) and they control how much or little you know about them (via their web page or the fact that you do not have acquaintances in common). They even control every aspect of their appearance since they can send you a copy of anyone's picture. You cannot be overly cautious in these situations and no one who is being honest with you would expect you to do otherwise. Be careful about divulging personal information about yourself. If you do decide to meet someone in person that you have met on the net, take a good friend along and meet only during the day in a busy, public setting.

Is the Information on the Net Reliable?

The quality of the information on the net varies just as it does everywhere else. The constitutional protections of freedom of the press and freedom of speech are not restricted to truthful or accurate statements. You should assume that anyone can say or write anything on the web. Offensive and sexually explicit material does exist on the net. If you wish to block your access to such material, programs exist that will prevent your browser from retrieving pages from known sources of such material. Since we do not all agree on what is offensive, these programs may require some fine tuning on your part.

While we each recognize pretty quickly what offends us, we do not as readily recognize misleading or false information. In order to use the net effectively you must develop your critical facilities so that you can distinguish reliable from misleading information. The late Carl Sagan referred to this skill as "The Fine Art of Baloney Detection." It takes practice and as you might guess there are web pages that will help you learn about how to evaluate web pages (for example <u>Internet Detective</u>[7]). Other good pages are <u>Critical Thinking Resources</u>[8] at Longview Community College and <u>A Student's Guide to WWW Research: Web Searching, Web Page Evaluation, and Research Strategies</u>[9] by Craig Branham.

Welcome to Internet Detective

an interactive tutorial on evaluating the quality of Internet

Internet Detective

Four characteristics are usually cited as important in evaluating print journalism. They apply equally well to web pages. They include the **source** of the information, the **objectivity** of the author, the **logic** of the argument, and **independent sources** of support for the argument or claim.

The **source** of the information includes the author and the publisher of the web page or pages. In some cases they will be the same person. The fact that someone is an expert on a particular topic does not mean they are always correct, but it does indicate that they have spent considerable time studying and researching the topic. They are likely to have considered many alternative explanations and are likely to make appropriate judgements regarding relevant versus irrelevant facts. Authority is limited, however. A world-recognized authority on particle physics is not necessarily an authority on anything else. In print journalism, an important role of the publisher is to provide fact-checking and independent verification of the claims made by authors. In professional journals, articles are reviewed by other authorities before they are published. However, on the net, it is not always easy to determine if there has been any independent evaluation of information. News organizations who depend on their reputations for accurate reporting are likely to have conducted some level of review on the material distributed on their web sites and some technical journals use peer reviews for articles published on the web. In most other cases, the fact that an organization hosts a web page should not be considered as evidence that the material on the page has been reviewed or verified by anyone. In some cases it may be difficult to determine the author of a web page. If there is no information about the author, you should be more skeptical of the accuracy of the material.

Another clue to the reliability of information is the **objectivity** of the author. There are very few topics about which everyone in the world agrees. Look to see if the author is attempting to be objective and present both sides of the issue or is advocating one side. Some web pages are clearly intended to advocate a particular viewpoint with no effort to consider other sides of an issue. Such pages can be a source of information for the point of view presented, but should not be used as a source of information for other points of view (find other web pages advocating those points of view). Watch out for a tendency in advocacy pages to dismiss counter arguments or to demean people who do not hold the view being presented.

You should also examine the **logic** of the arguments presented by the author. Ask yourself if the argument makes sense. Can you see simple alternative explanations that have been ignored or overlooked? Make certain that the arguments are complete enough for you to see how each step leads to the next one. Watch out for over-generalization where the author convinces you that a claim holds in one case, therefore it must be universally true. Also watch out for "burden of proof" tricks where the author tries to shift the burden of proof to the other side (e.g. "although many claims of visitation by extraterrestrials have been proven false, how could they all be false?"). Other tricks involve dismissing opposing viewpoints by questioning their proponents' motives (*ad hominem* attacks) or criticizing an extreme version of an opposing viewpoint that no one would support (straw man arguments).

Statistics also provide opportunities to mislead. There are several common techniques for misdirection. One involves using raw counts rather than rates. For example, "evidence of our more violent society is provided by the fact that the number of homicides increased 50% from 1970 to 1990." Of course population increased as well. There was an increase in homicide rates, but it was about 20% not 50%. A second trick involves ignoring control groups, "in a large sample, 18% of the people who ate olestra (a fat substitute) complained of some form of stomach distress the following day." True, but almost 20% of the control group who did not eat olestra also complained of stomach distress. Finally, watch out for confusion of correlation with causation. Just because two variables increase over time, it does not follow that one causes the other. They could both be caused by a third factor which was not measured in the study. For example, population growth ("The need for gun control is demonstrated by the fact that the number of homicides committed in a city is directly correlated with the number of guns sold.").

Finally, you should consider **independent sources** of information that support or fail to support the claims made on the page. Are you aware of opposing views or information that are not mentioned on the web page? If so, you should be skeptical of the author's authority and doubt his or her objectivity. Check to see if the author provides references for factual claims or arguments. Search the web to look for other web pages that would support or contradict the claims made by the author. You should consider the evaluation of information to be a process not an event. As you find out more and more about a topic, use your new information to reevaluate materials you encountered earlier.

Where Should I Start?

When you start your web browser, a hypertext page loads automatically. That page is your **start page**. The default start page is usually located at the web site of the company that produced the web browser. You can change the start page at any time by changing the site listed in your preferences. You can create a small web page of your own and load it from your own computer. It can be little more than a list or a table containing the pages you most often like to visit. Alternatively you can customize the default start page or specify that another site will be your start page. **Web portal** sites provide a wide variety of information in a compact format including news, stock quotes, a search engine, a subject classification of the web and more. You customize the page to include particular kinds of news (e.g. only sports), particular stocks, your favorite web pages, and more. You may also be able to chat with other people who are currently online, set up an email account, or even a web page at your portal site. MyYahoo![10] By Yahoo! and MSN[11] by Microsoft are examples.

Topical Guides. Most subjects have guides to the web. For anthropology try the following: Anthropology Resources on the Internet[12] written by Bernard Clist. The World Wide Web Virtual Library: Anthropology[13] is maintained by AnthroTech. The World Wide Web Virtual Library: Archaeology (ARCHNET)[14] is maintained by Arizona State University. At About.com[15] guides review interesting web sites and give suggestions. The Archaeology[16] guide is Kris Hirst.

Wadsworth Welcome to Anthropology Online provides information about anthropology, the web, and Wadsworth texts. You can find it at Anthropology Online.[17]

Web Rings. A good way to begin browsing the web if you don't have a clear idea of what you want to find is to use a web ring. Web rings are collections of related web sites. Each site in the web ring has a link to the site before it and the site after it in the list. Often the site also has a way to randomly select a site from the web ring. The main web site for web rings is Welcome to WebRing![18] Here you will find information about web rings and how to create them. You will also find subject classifications for the existing web rings and a search function that will let you search for web rings that have a particular word or phrase in their title or description. Below are several web rings that relate to anthropology. Adding a site to a web ring is completely voluntary and you may find sites that do not really seem to fit, but this is a good way to begin to surf the net.

- Anthropology Web Ring[19] (48 sites) is a collection of Anthropology Web Pages on the Internet.
- Archaeology on the Net[20] (349 sites) aims to provide a resources guide for archaeology related sites on the Internet.
- Archaeology Ring[21] (81 sites) includes many sites with archaeological content. All these sites belong to associations or foundations which perform or describe archaeological excavations. Field Work servers are welcome on this ring, too. There is no limitation regarding the period; the range is from prehistorical, proto-historical, and classical up to modern industry archaeology.
- The Paleo Ring[22] (187 sites) is a developing collection of Websites that promote Paleontology, Paleoanthropology, Prehistoric Archeology, The Evolution of Behavior, and Evolutionary Biology in general. Take a ride through the past and learn how life as we know it came to be. The goal is to develop this ring into a valuable tool for education.
- Ring of Languages & Linguistics[23] (87 sites) is for anyone interested in languages or linguistics. Sites in the ring relate in some way to either languages or linguistics. This could also include anything about invented languages as well.
- The Ring of Folklore and Urban Legends[24] (67 sites) includes sites about folklore: urban legends, ghost stories, folk tales, riddles, and

jokes. There may be discussions of how stories spread from one place to another, how they change over time, and what, if any, truth there is to them.

Web Links

1. Netscape: http://browsers.netscape.com/
2. Internet Explorer: http://www.microsoft.com/windows/ie/
3. Acrobat Reader: http://www.adobe.com/prodindex/acrobat/readstep.html
4. Windows Media Player: http://www.microsoft.com/windows/mediaplayer/default.asp
5. RealOne Player: http://www.real.com/
6. QuickTime: http://www.apple.com/quicktime/
7. Internet Detective: http://sosig.ac.uk/desire/internet-detective.html
8. Critical Thinking Resources: http://www.kcmetro.cc.mo.us/longview/ctac/toc.htm
9. A Student's Guide to WWW Research: Web Searching, Web Page Evaluation, and Research Strategies: http://www.slu.edu/departments/english/research/
10. Yahoo!: http://www.yahoo.com/
11. MSN.COM: http://home.microsoft.com/
12. Anthropology Resources on the Internet: http://home.worldnet.fr/clist/Anthro/index.html
13. World Wide Web Virtual Library: Anthropology: http://www.anthrotech.com/resources/
14. World Wide Web Virtual Library: Archaeology (ARCHNET): http://archnet.asu.edu/archnet/
15. About.com: http://www.about.com/
16. Archaeology: http://archaeology.about.com/
17. Anthropology Online: http://www.wadsworth.com/anthropology_d/
18. Welcome to WebRing!: http://www.webring.com/
19. Anthropology Web Ring: http://www.webring.org/cgi-bin/webring?ring = anthropology;list
20. Archaeology on the Net: http://www.webring.org/cgi-bin/webring?ring = archonnet;list

21. Archaeology Ring: http://www.webring.org/cgi-bin/webring?ring = archeoring;list

22. The Paleo Ring: http://www.webring.org/cgi-bin/webring?ring = paleoring;list

23. Ring of Languages & Linguistics: http://www.webring.org/cgi-bin/webring?ring = lang;list

24. The Ring of Folklore and Urban Legends: http://www.webring.org/cgi-bin/webring?ring = urbanlegends;list

Communicating

Email

Electronic mail and variations of it are the most heavily used aspect of the net. Like regular mail, your message travels to the person you have sent it to and waits to be retrieved and read. It has most of the advantages of regular mail, but it arrives at its destination much faster. One disadvantage of email is that you do not receive any confirmation that the message was read and many people still don't read their email regularly. If you receive a message from someone that you do not communicate with regularly, it doesn't hurt to respond with a simple note that you received the message.

When you get a computer account, you will also get an email address. It will be something like "jsmith@bigu.edu." The part of your email address to the left of the "@" sign is your account name while the part on the right is the **domain name**. The domain name is used to route messages to a particular computer that saves the message in a directory associated with a particular account. The message stays in the directory until you retrieve, read, or delete it. There are two basic ways of handling email accounts. One involves using email software on your personal computer to retrieve all of the new messages from your mail account. You can then read, save, reply, or do whatever you want with each message. Generally the messages are deleted from the computer that stores the messages until you retrieve them. This is convenient if you want to store messages without worrying about using up the space allotted for your email account. The second way is to leave messages on your email account until you delete them. This is convenient if you access your email from different computers (at your campus computer lab or while traveling). You should remember that your messages occupy space on the computer that holds your email account and you have probably been allocated only a certain amount of space. If you receive many messages or a few big messages (with large files attached), your space allocation will fill up and any further messages will be returned to the sender. You may not receive any message when this occurs. For this reason, download your email regularly (method one) or check your email regularly and delete messages you no longer need (method two).

In order to send a message to someone, you need to know their email address. While you can often find it by using some of the search engines on the web, it is usually easiest to ask for the address or have the person send you a message. If you attend a university, there will probably be a phonebook of email addresses on the university web page. When you send a message, include information on the subject line that will let the recipient know what the message is about. Due to spam and the possibility of receiving a virus by email, increasingly people are deleting messages without reading them if they come from strangers or have blank or suspicious subject lines. Most email programs also allow you to add a signature to the bottom of your email message. The signature can provide additional information about you such as your name, phone number, occupation, or web page. You can also delete the signature when you are replying to a message or sending mail to someone you know.

Electronic mail introduces old problems in a new guise, such as, spam or electronic junk mail. People are still learning how to communicate by electronic mail. Many of the non-verbal cues that we use to evaluate what someone is saying are missing: the smile or wink that indicates a remark is intended to be humorous or sarcastic; the hesitation or stress in someone's voice that suggests a reply that might not be completely truthful; the flow of someone's handwriting as a clue to his or her emotional state. In addition, we lose the cues that tell us about the impact of our own words: the frown or scowl that indicates that our words have been interpreted as a threat or insult. Finally, electronic mail makes it easy to communicate with complete strangers who don't know anything about you (such as your sense of humor). Messages that depend on nonverbal qualities are often misunderstood in electronic communication. Sarcasm usually fails. It is easy to respond without thinking, and impossible to take the message back after it has been sent. A second element of electronic communication is that we have not yet developed effective filters for the flow of information. We are accustomed to filtering (ignoring) irrelevant information from television and radio, junk mail, and people around us without giving it much thought. Irrelevant electronic mail messages seem to provoke more hostility than irrelevant information from sources with which we are more accustomed. The best thing about irrelevant email is that the lost disk space is easily recycled by simply deleting the message.

Because you respond to someone without seeing them (and they do not see you when they respond) it is easier to ignore simple courtesies and respond in an insulting or offensive manner. Read messages you have composed from beginning to end, before you send them. If you receive an insulting message, delete it and resist the temptation to reply with equal venom. You will not teach the other person a lesson and you will simply make yourself a target for further insults. Develop the ability to shrug off minor insults without dwelling on them. It will serve you well later in life. Remember that the net is decentralized and chaotic. For more helpful hints on email Netiquette visit the <u>Netiquette Home Page</u>[1].

If you receive threatening messages, do not delete them. Save them and forward copies to the system administrators (sysop) of the domain from which the threatening messages are coming. The domain is the part of the email address to the right of the "@" site. There is no standard email address for systems operators so you may have to try several ("sysop@Site.com" or "postmaster@" or "security@" or "abuse@"). Do not delete the message as your copy may contain additional information that your email software did not include in the forwarded copy. Also contact the sysop of you Internet provider or university computer center to get their advice and assistance on how to proceed.

Mailing Lists

Mailing lists make it easy to participate in a discussion with many other people. When you subscribe to a mailing list, you are asking to receive a copy of every message sent to the list. The messages will arrive as email. There are mailing lists covering nearly every conceivable topic. <u>Topica</u>[2] maintains an index to 90,000 mailing lists where you can search for ones of interest to you. If you want to limit your search to anthropology lists, look at Bernard Clist's <u>Anthropology Resources on the Internet</u>[3] for some ideas. If the list has a web page to provide access to its archives, you can browse previously posted messages to see if the topics discussed interest you.

There are several kinds of lists. Some are restricted and some are not. Restricted lists require the permission of the listowner to subscribe. These lists are used for groups of people who are collaborating on some project and wish to restrict the use of the list very narrowly. For example, your instructor may create a mailing list for a course you are taking and subscription to the list would be limited to those in the class. Lists can also be moderated or unmoderated. In a moderated list, the listowner reviews posts before they are distributed. Moderated lists provide a further check on messages before they are distributed so that only messages on the list topic are distributed. Unmoderated lists allow subscribers to post directly to the list. This speeds up the discussion, but it may result in a higher number of off-topic messages.

If you are new to email, subscribing to a list is a good way to begin receiving email. Some lists generate many messages (50-100 per day) while other lists generate many fewer messages. A general rule of thumb is that the more general the topic and the more subscribers, the more messages per day. If you subscribe to a busy list you should check your email daily since once the disk space assigned to your account fills, every message will be returned to the sender or to the listowner (or both). If this happens, you may be removed from the list. You can subscribe again once you have cleared your mailbox. Once you have found a list that you are interested in, you will need to learn how to subscribe. Most of the mailing lists are managed by one of three computer programs: listproc, listserv, or majordomo. Completely in accord with the chaos that is the net, they use somewhat different methods of subscribing and unsubscribing:

LISTPROC

1. To subscribe send an email message to listproc@DomainName containing the message

    SUBSCRIBE ListName YourFirstName YourLastName

2. To leave the list send an email message to listproc@DomainName containing the message

    UNSUBSCRIBE ListName

3. To get information about other commands send an email message to listproc@DomainName containing the message

    HELP

LISTSERV

1. To subscribe send an email message to listserv@Domain containing the message

    SUB ListName YourFirstName YourLastName

2. To leave the list send an email message to listserv@Domain containing the message

    SIGNOFF ListName

3. To get further details send an email message to listserv@Domain containing the message

    HELP

MAJORDOMO

1. To subscribe send an email message to majordomo@Domain containing the message

    SUBSCRIBE ListName

2. To leave the list send an email message to majordomo@Domain containing the message

    UNSUBSCRIBE ListName

3. To get further details send an email message to majordomo@Domain containing the message

    HELP

To subscribe to a list you need to know the list email address and what kind it is. If the list called NEWBIE@BigTimeUniversity.edu is a listserv list, you would send the following message:

    sub NEWBIE YourFirstName YourLastName

to listserv@BigTimeUniversity.edu.

There are some web pages that allow you to subscribe to a list from the web. Follow the instructions and you will be added to the list. The program will send you a standard welcome message with instructions about the list and the list software. Keep this message since you will probably want to refer to it later (and it tells you how to unsubscribe from the list).

Your fellow subscribers on the list make up a limited community. They are not your friends (maybe eventually, but not automatically) and they are not a resource at your beck and call. List communities generally consist of a core of long-term subscribers and others who have recently joined the list. You can avoid the classic "newbie" mistakes by heeding ten simple rules:

1. Know to whom you are replying. Pay close attention to the "To:" field on the email messages you are composing. Some lists are configured so that when you use the "Reply" function, the message goes to the entire list. Others set the "Reply" function so that the message goes only to the person who sent the message. There are good reasons for each method, but it is easy to get them confused. Once you have learned the soft-

ware, you will know how to send messages to the whole list if the default is to the sender and vice versa.

2. The list subscribers are not a replacement for the library. Do not ask for help with your homework or research paper unless you have exhausted the available resources first. Then ask very specific questions, not "Can anyone tell me about the Moundbuilders?"

3. Do not post test messages or "Hi" messages to the list. Send test messages to your friends or to yourself (your email program will not object if you send a message to yourself). Especially on a large list, many subscribers come and go all the time.

4. Do not quote someone's message, add "I agree" or "I disagree," and then post it back to the list. The list is for discussion, not for voting. The general rule of thumb is that your contribution should be longer than the part of the message you quote.

5. Never, Ever, Ever send your list commands to the mailing list. More sophisticated programs will simply return them to you (often with cryptic error messages), but if it gets through, all of the list subscribers will see that you don't know what you are doing. On top of that, the mailing list program does not monitor the list for commands so it will never see your command.

6. Don't play Paul Revere. There are many pseudo virus alerts that circulate around the net. The "Good Times" virus hoax is the most famous, but there are many others. They circulate on a six to twelve month cycle so once you've been on the net for a year you will have run across most of them. If someone sends you an alert, check it out on the web first (e.g. Symantech's Anti Virus Reference Center[4] or McAfee.com Anti Virus[5]). The U.S. Department of Energy Computer Incident Advisory Capability[6] is also a good reference. CIAC's Hoaxbusters[7] page describes common Internet hoaxes.

7. Do not post humorous jokes, stories, or riddles to the mailing list unless that is the topic of the list. Just like the virus hoaxes, most of these have been around for a long time. Also recognize that you are communicating with many different people all over the world and there is a good chance that not only is your story off-topic, it may also be offensive to someone. In anthropology the story about the hominid fossil that turns out to be a Barbie doll has been around long enough that it has its own web pages

(see if you can find them). For other tired stories visit the <u>Urban Legends Archive</u>[8] or the <u>Urban Legends Reference Page</u>[9].

8. Stay out of flame wars. A flame is an antagonistic or insulting reply. On mailing lists you will meet some of the nicest people in the world. People who will go out of their way to help you with a problem or help you work out the details of an argument you are trying to develop. They will help you even though it is not their job and they will receive no compensation or credit for doing it. You will also find people who are not so generous. People who like to post outrageous statements just in order to see who will take the bait. Don't take the bait and don't respond. It is very unlikely that the person who sent the message is naive or will respond to gentle criticism (or any criticism for that matter).

9. Don't publicly point out people's mistakes. You will make plenty as you are getting started on the net, and you will appreciate people who send you a message privately rather than posting it to the entire list.

10. Finally, when it doubt, just observe. When you first join a list that has been established for a long time, spend a few weeks or a month getting an idea of the ebb and flow of topics and how the subscribers interact. If you have a question, try to locate an archive for the list (a searchable database of previous posts) to see if it has already been answered.

Distribution lists are one-way mailing lists. You generally subscribe via a form on the web page of the organization that is managing the list. You cannot post to a distribution list, it is just a channel for the organization to send you information, offers, special sale notices, breaking news events, etc. As you are visiting web pages you will run across many opportunities to subscribe to distribution lists. Subscribe to those you want, but if you subscribe to too many you will find your mailbox full, sometimes with material that looks very similar to junk mail. Some distribution lists send messages only every once in a while, while others (especially news agencies) send messages every day. The message usually contains instructions for removing your address from the list.

Newsgroups

Newsgroups are similar to bulletin boards. The original USENET newsgroups were developed early in the history of the Internet and were expanded and reorganized in 1986 ("The Great Renaming"). You do not actually subscribe to a newsgroup, although that fact is often unclear because the software for reading and posting to newsgroups has commands for "subscribing." Actually, "monitoring" would be a better term. The messages on a bulletin board stay on the computer systems of your university or ISP until you retrieve them. When you use your software to "subscribe" to a newsgroup, you are only telling the software to check that group for new messages. You can download all of the new messages in a group or just retrieve the subject lines from the messages to see if any are interesting enough to retrieve. To unsubscribe, you simply tell your software to stop downloading the messages from that group. Newsgroups do not have owners or moderators (except in a few cases) and no one knows when you subscribe or unsubscribe. Newsgroups are a good way to monitor subjects that you are generally interested in, but do not want to receive every message every person sends. Since you do not actually receive the messages, you have to visit the group regularly as messages last only a day or a week depending on how much traffic there is on the group. You may be able to find missed messages at Google Groups[10] where many newsgroups are archived.

Newsgroups are organized around a loose hierarchy. Groups that begin with "comp." are about computers, networks, and software. Groups that begin with "rec." are about recreational activities, "sci." groups cover science, "soc." groups are about social groups and society, "talk." groups are for wide ranging discussion and debate about topics that often trigger passionate responses. Groups beginning with "alt." (Alternate) overlap with the other groups. The group started out as a renegade hierarchy for topics that were originally banned from USENET. Sexually explicit groups are present in the "alt." hierarchy, but so are groups on many other topics. In addition to USENET, there are also newsgroups maintained by major software companies. These newsgroups provide a means for people to ask for assistance and to make suggestions about new features or new products.

There thousands of newsgroups archived by Google Groups including over 700 million messages, but there are also regional and local groups bringing the total even higher. However, you really only need to know about the groups that are available from your ISP or university. Most will offer access to some newsgroups, but do not offer access to all of them. Maintaining storage space and access for newsgroups is costly so ISPs and universities limit access to their local users. Once you have configured your software to connect to the newsgroup server (if your university is myu.edu, the newsgroup server will often be news.myu.edu), you can retrieve the list of newsgroups carried by your system. Once you have the list, you can select the ones you want to "subscribe" to, but recall that the subscription is only a way of telling your software to check for new messages to that group whenever you check for new newsgroup messages. There are also corporate newsgroups that provide software support. For example, point your web browser to news://news.microsoft.com and you should get a listing of over one thousand news groups relating to Microsoft© software.

Chat and Instant Messaging

In 1988 the ability to link several people together so that they could simultaneously send messages to one another instantaneously (**chat**) was devised. Commercial network services such as Compuserve and America Online already had this capability. Internet Relay Chat (IRC) has expanded in size and flexibility and, to some degree, has been captured by the web. IRC is like a conference call except that everyone has to type what they want to say. Since you need to type quickly to keep up, people use a great variety of acronyms to express things compactly (for example, imho -"in my humble opinion" and rotfl "rolling on the floor laughing"). There are now two ways to chat. The first is through an IRC server that handles hundreds of separate chat rooms (or channels). In order to contact them you need IRC client software (for example Microsoft Chat, available free from Microsoft). After you log into a server, you select the room you want to enter. The second way is through a web site that offers chat capabilities inside your web browser. For these you may not need any additional software or the site may download a program that will work inside your browser to handle the chat features. Yahoo! Chat[11] and MSNBC Chat[12] are two examples. You will have to register before you will be able to chat by providing a handle or alias (the name you want to be known by in the chat room) and your email address.

Most chats are simply collections of people who have come together to discuss a particular topic. There is no moderator and no way to keep the discussion on a particular topic. If you find yourself in a room with someone who makes you uncomfortable, just exit the room. Other chat rooms have moderators who keep the discussion on topic and can disconnect people who are offensive or obscene. Finally, some chats are organized around a celebrity guest. In these chats, you will probably need to submit your question to a moderator to get it passed on to the celebrity guest. Your instructor may use chat sessions to allow people to discuss a topic outside class or to allow you to chat with anthropology students in another class (or university). Before getting started you should look at Internet Relay Chat (IRC) Help[13] and Chat Etiquette/Chat Protocol[14].

Instant messaging or paging allows you to send a message to another person who is online as long as that person is running compatible software. The message generally arrives more quickly than email and the software will tell you if the other person is online. The concept was first popularized by a program called ICQ[15] ("I seek you"). AOL Instant Messenger[16] (America Online) and .net MSN Messenger[17] (Microsoft) are the most popular and are freely available to anyone. Ask your anthropology instructor if he or she uses instant messaging. It can be a quick way to get an answer to a question while studying for an exam.

Web Links

1. Netiquette Home Page:
   http://www.fau.edu/netiquette/netiquette.html

2. Topica: http://www.topica.com/

3. Anthropology Resources on the Internet:
   http://home.worldnet.fr/clist/Anthro/index.html

4. Symantech's Anti Virus Reference Center:
   http://www.symantec.com/avcenter/index.html

5. McAfee.com Anti Virus: http://www.mcafee.com/anti-virus/

6. Computer Incident Advisory Capability:
   http://ciac.llnl.gov/ciac/CIACHome.html

7. Hoaxbusters: http://hoaxbusters.ciac.org/

8. Urban Legends Archive: http://www.urbanlegends.com/

9. Urban Legends Reference Page: http://www.snopes2.com/

10. DejaNews: http://www.deja.com/usenet/

11. Yahoo! Chat: http://chat.yahoo.com/

12. MSNBC Chat: http://www.msnbc.com/chat/default.asp

13. Internet Relay Chat (IRC) Help: http://www.irchelp.org/

14. Chat Etiquette/Chat Protocol:
    http://www.minopher.net.au/WebEd/protocol.htm

15. ICQ: http://web.icq.com/

16. AOL Instant Messenger: http://www.aim.com/

17. .net MSN Messenger: http://messenger.msn.com/

Simple Searches

With an estimated one billion pages and counting, it can be difficult to find exactly what you want on the web. You can reduce the time it takes by analyzing what you are looking for. If you are looking for web sites that focus on a particular subject, your best option is to use a web site that classifies many sites by subject. If you are looking for specific facts and figures, try an encyclopedia or a reference desk. If these don't work or your question is very specific, try a web search engine.

Web Site Classifications

Many searches involve fairly general questions such as "What web sites are there on anthropology (or ethnomusicology)?" or "What web sites provide information on genealogy?" These kinds of questions are best answered by web sites that have classified a large number of web sites into subject categories and by topical guides to the web. The original subject classification of the web is Yahoo![1] It begins by dividing web sites into 14 categories ranging from "Arts & Humanities" to "News & Media" to "Society & Culture." Each of these categories is subdivided and subdivided again so that you can browse for increasingly specific kinds of sites. Yahoo! searches the subject categories as well as the web page titles and their descriptions. Yahoo! gathers information about new web sites from many sources and the creators of web sites usually notify Yahoo! of new web sites to add to the classification. Another good subject classification is the Open Directory Project[2]. A good guide for academic topics is the UniGuide Academic Guide to the Internet[3]. Using a subject classification web site is similar to the subject classification of your library catalog. You will find books relating to specific topics, but you will not necessarily find where a particular fact is located in the book.

The founders of the World Wide Web realized that information distributed all over the globe would be difficult to find unless there were some guides. They created the World Wide Web Virtual Library[4] by selecting volunteers to catalog major web sites for various subjects. If you look at the list of subjects, you will see that some categories are quite broad while others are quite specific. Since they are produced by volunteers whose workload varies, they may or may not be completely up-to-date. They are a good place to start, and often the sites are described more completely than the single line descriptions in Yahoo! Another useful resource for broad subject searches is the Argus Clearinghouse[5]. Throughout the web, people have spent time collecting information about web sites, mailing lists, and newsgroups. They compile this information into documents that are stored on the web and updated. The Argus Clearinghouse helps you to find these documents by cataloging them according to subject area, and by providing a summary and rating for each one.

For anthropology there are a number of subject guides. The best include the following: <u>Anthropology Resources on the Internet</u>[6] Bernard Clist; the <u>World Wide Web Virtual Library: Anthropology</u>[7] by AnthroTech; and the <u>World Wide Web Virtual Library: Archaeology (ARCHNET)</u>[8] at Arizona State University.

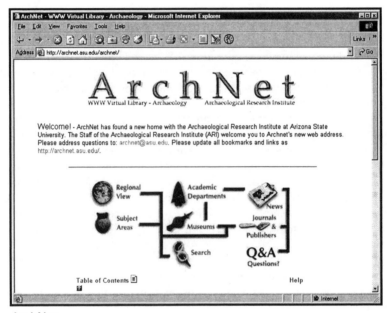

ArchNet

Facts and Figures

If you want to know the current ruler of a particular country or the population of the world explore one of the virtual reference desks or encyclopedias. A spectacular resource is <u>Encyclopedia Britannica</u>[9] which provides the full text of the encyclopedia and links to other resources on the web. <u>My Virtual Reference Desk</u>[10] and <u>Martindale's 'The Reference Desk'</u>[11] are the most extensive and complete of the reference desks.

You will find links to a broad range of sources for factual information. Information Please[12] allows you to search its almanac, dictionary, and encyclopedia. Two good sources of information on other countries are the United Nations Infonation[13] by the UN (although the interface takes some practice) and A+ Country Reports[14]. A good source of maps is National Geographic's Map Machine[15]. Anthropology Biography[16] and Biography.com[17] provide capsule biographies for many of your favorite anthropologists. The Ethnographic Atlas[18] at the University of Kent provides summary descriptions of about 60 societies.

Government publications, such as the CIA World Factbook[19] and the the Library of Congress Country Studies Series[20] are also available. From the U.S. Census you can download the tables from the Statistical Abstract of the U.S.[21] in Adobe Acrobat format.

Web Search Engines

As you become more specific about the information you want to find, you will probably turn to one of the search engines on the web that have indexed millions of web pages. Imagine if all the indexes from all the books in the library were combined into a single giant index. You could then find not only the book, but also the page you wanted in a single search. That is what search engines try to do. While Yahoo! classifies web sites, search engines index web pages. Most search engines also provide subject categories of web sites so that the difference between the two is blurring.

The indexes are constructed by software robots that travel around the web 24 hours a day discovering and indexing web pages. The coverage that each search engine offers is slightly different. Some try to be as comprehensive as possible, but no one engine has indexed all of the web pages. Google[22] is the current champion with about 1.5 billion pages indexed. It is currently the most popular search engine because the results of its searches tend to rank the results so that the pages you are looking for are more likely to be near the top of the list. AltaVista Search[23] and Fast Search[24] are second with over 500 million pages indexed. Ixquick[25] and Vivisimo[26] send your query to several search engines and then combines the results. If you do not include several terms in your search, you will end up with thousands of pages containing the term you searched for. Each search engine has methods of restricting the search and each search engine has ways of ranking the results according to those that should be most useful to you. You should experiment with several. Some allow only relatively simple searches while others allow you to construct complex boolean queries (you can find out what these are under Help on one of the big search engine home pages). NorthernLight[27] allows you to search a database of articles from journals in addition to searching web pages. You can then also purchase a copy of the article if it is not in your local library.

Web Links

1. Yahoo!: http://www.yahoo.com/

2. Open Directory Project: http://dmoz.org/

3. UniGuide Academic Guide to the Internet: http://www.aldea.com/guides/ag/attframes2.html

4. World Wide Web Virtual Library: http://www.vlib.org/

5. Argus Clearinghouse: http://www.clearinghouse.net/

6. Anthropology Resources on the Internet: http://home.worldnet.fr/clist/Anthro/index.html

7. World Wide Web Virtual Library: Anthropology: http://vlib.anthrotech.com/

8. World Wide Web Virtual Library: Archaeology (ARCHNET): http://archnet.asu.edu/archnet/

9. Encyclopedia Britannica: http://www.britannica.com/

10. My Virtual Reference Desk: http://www.refdesk.com/

11. Martindale's 'The Reference Desk': http://www-sci.lib.uci.edu/HSG/Ref.html

12. Information Please Almanac: http://www.infoplease.com/index.html

13. Infonation: http://www.un.org/Pubs/CyberSchoolBus/infonation/e_infonation.htm

14. A+ Country Reports: http://www.countryreports.org/

15. Map Machine: http://www.nationalgeographic.com/resources/ngo/maps/

16. Anthropology Biography: http://www.anthro.mankato.msus.edu/information/biography/index.shtml

17. Biography.com: http://www.biography.com/

18. Ethnographic Atlas: http://lucy.ukc.ac.uk/EthnoAtlas/ethno.html

19. CIA World Factbook: http://www.odci.gov/cia/publications/factbook/index.html

20. Country Studies Series: http://lcweb2.loc.gov/frd/cs/cshome.html

21. Statistical Abstract of the U.S.:
     http://www.census.gov/statab/www/

22. Google: http://www.google.com/

23. AltaVista: http://www.altavista.com/

24. Fast Search: http://www.alltheweb.com/

25. Ixquick: http://www.ixquick.com/

26. Vivisimo: http://vivisimo.com/

27. NorthernLight: http://www.northernlight.com/

Research on the Web

The World Wide Web can help you improve your understanding of anthropology by supplementing lectures, providing a context for the examples in the text, making you aware of current events that relate to the topics discussed in the text and in class, and by giving you tools to increase the productivity of your research. The web is not a replacement for your campus library, but it can provide you with ready access to a great variety of information such as up-to-date statistics, maps, photos, or greater detail about topics covered briefly in the text. You can also query library catalogs (probably the catalog on your campus) to check the availability of books and articles.

Library Catalogs

Many colleges and universities have made their catalogs available for online access. While some may require a special program to access, increasingly they are designed for use with any web browser. The Academic Libraries[1] web index at Yahoo! includes nearly 500 academic libraries around the world including Harvard University and Cambridge University. LibWeb[2] is even more comprehensive, listing 6000 libraries in 100 countries. These catalogs can help you locate books in your campus library and can help you find references that are not available locally (so that you can request them through interlibrary loan). Library catalogs are a good place to find out what resources are available for a term paper topic or a presentation. Often they will also tell you if the book you need is checked out and when it is due back to the library.

Not really a library catalog, but nearly as useful are the web pages for booksellers such as Amazon[3]. If the book is no longer in print, try the used book search engines such as abebooks.com[4] and Book Finder[5]. These sites allow you to search for books that are currently out of print. They often provide a picture of the cover of the book and may include review comments and a table of contents. This can be particularly helpful if the book you need is not at your library and you don't have enough time to get it through interlibrary loan.

Online Books

A number of books and articles are available directly on the Internet. You can download them to a disk and read them at your leisure. While reading a book on a computer screen is not as pleasant as reading a physical book, it does have one advantage. With an online book, you can search for any word or phrase. This is useful if you think that the author mentions a topic that you are interested in, but you don't want to read the whole book to find a single phrase or paragraph. Because of copyright restrictions, most online books are older books whose copyright has expired. It is a good place to look for works that are primarily of historical interest such as the works of Charles Darwin, Herbert Spencer, or Karl Marx. The Internet Public Library[6] and The Online Books Page[7] let you search thousands of online titles including books and shorter pieces. For books relating to the United States, try Making of America[8], a collection of 1,600 books and 50,000 articles relating to American social history published during the nineteenth century.

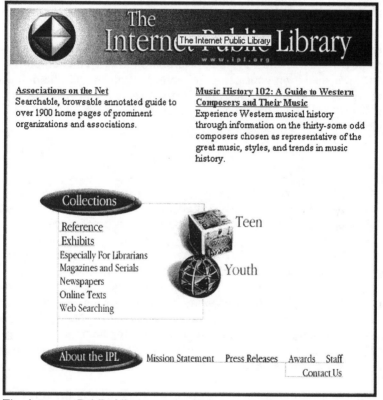

The Internet Public Library

To locate recently published articles relating to a particular topic, check Ingenta[9], a database of current article information taken from well over 25,000 publications. NorthernLight[10] allows you to search for magazine articles and order copies over the web. Recently the Royal Anthropological Institute started The Anthropological Index Online[11]. The Centre for Social Anthropology and Computing at the University of Kent has a searchable Anthropology Bibliography[12] that covers the field of Social Anthropology in the broadest sense. Other indices such as the Social Sciences Periodical Index or Current Contents on the web are available as subscription services. However, many academic libraries subscribe to these services so you may be able to search them by connecting to your university library web page.

More and more university libraries are subscribing to electronic versions of professional journals. Electronic versions of a journal allow you to download an article in Adobe Acrobat® format. You can print out the article or read it on your computer screen. You should find out what journals your library gets in electronic format since it can save you a trip to the library and the information is available 24 hours a day, 7 days a week.

Writing Resources

When you have to write a paper, there are several web resources that can help answer your questions about grammar and style, copyright and fair use, and how to cite digital information. A great place to start is Duskin/ McGraw's How to Write Term Papers[13] written by John T. Rourke. The 1918 version of *The Elements of Style,*[14] a classic manual on writing by William Strunk, is available on the Net. For questions about grammar you can try two different handbooks on the web. The Grammar Handbook[15] at the University of Illinois Urbana Champaign and the On-Line English Grammar[16] by the Digital Education Network. A good collection of writing and reference tools for anthropologists is Writing Tools for Anthropology Students[17] compiled by Michael Dean Murphy at the University of Alabama.

If an idea is not yours you need to cite its source. Dartmouth College has a nice web site called Sources: Their Use and Acknowledgment[18] that will give you the basics. How do you cite electronic resources? The American Psychological Association offers guidelines for citing electronic publications in Electronic Reference Formats[19]. Also very useful is the style guide of the American Anthropological Association at AAA Style Guide[20].

If you need more details about copyright and fair use, try the U.S. Copyright Office, FAQ[21] page with answers to your frequently asked questions as well.

Web Links

1. Academic Libraries:
    http://www.yahoo.com/Reference/Libraries/Academic_Libraries/
2. LibWeb: http://sunsite.berkeley.edu/Libweb/
3. Amazon: http://www.amazon.com/
4. abebooks.com: http://www.abebooks.com/
5. Book Finder: http://www.bookfinder.com/
6. Internet Public Library: http://www.ipl.org/
7. The Online Books Page: http://onlinebooks.library.upenn.edu/
8. Making of America: http://www.umdl.umich.edu/moa/
9. Ingenta: http://www.ingenta.com/
10. NorthernLight: http://www.northernlight.com/
11. The Anthropological Index Online: http://lucy.ukc.ac.uk/AIO.html
12. Anthropology Bibliography: http://lucy.ukc.ac.uk/cgi-bin/uncgi/search_bib2/Makhzan
13. How to Write Term Papers:
    http://www.dushkin.com/online/study/dgen2.mhtml
14. *The Elements of Style*: http://www.bartleby.com/141/index.html
15. Grammar Handbook:
    http://www.english.uiuc.edu/cws/wworkshop/grammar_handbook.htm
16. On-Line English Grammar:
    http://www.edunet.com/english/grammar/index.html
17. Writing Tools for Anthropology Students:
    http://www.as.ua.edu/ant/libguidt.htm
18. Sources: Their Use and Acknowledgment:
    http://www.dartmouth.edu/~sources/index.html
19. Electronic Reference Formats:
    http://www.apastyle.org/elecref.html
20. AAA Style Guide: http://www.aaanet.org/pubs/style_guide.htm
21. U.S. Copyright Office, FAQ:
    http://lcweb.loc.gov/copyright/faq.html

Current Events

You can follow current events on the web by visiting the web pages of newspapers and broadcast news organizations. For national and world news my favorites are <u>ABC News</u>[1], <u>BBC News</u>[2], and <u>The New York Times</u>[3], but try others to see which ones you prefer. The New York Times requires that you register to browse the site, but registration is free. You can find an extensive listing of online U. S. papers at <u>US Newspaper Links</u>[4] and one that includes papers around the rest of the world at <u>Thousands of Newspaper on the Net</u>[5]. There are many other news sites on the web from all over the world. You should be able to locate them at Yahoo!

To find other news stories, you can visit a topical news page or use a news search engine. Topical news pages provide links to news items covering a particular subject. For links to news stories that relate to all aspects of anthropology visit <u>Anthropology in the News</u>[6]. This is a page I started several years ago to replace the news clippings that I placed on a bulletin board outside my office. The page provides about two months of news links in the Breaking News section and has archives going back about a year. Checking the page regularly will keep you up to date on the latest discoveries, research results, and world events that involve anthropology or anthropologists. Other topical news pages include <u>Artigen</u>[7] and <u>NewsHub</u>[8].

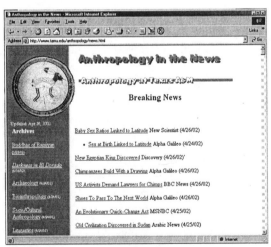

Anthropology in the News

News search engines allow you to search recent news stories that include a particular word or phrase in the title or in the text of the story. Most news web sites allow you to search their site, but some charge for retrieving older stories from their archives. There are a couple of search engines that search over several sites. These include NewsTracker[9] by Excite and TotalNews[10]

Web Links

1. ABC News: http://www.abcnews.com/
2. BBC News: http://news.bbc.co.uk/default.htm
3. The New York Times: http://www.nytimes.com/
4. US Newspaper Links: http://www.usnpl.com/
5. Thousands of Newspapers on the Net: http://www.onlinenewspapers.com/
6. Anthropology in the News: http://www.tamu.edu/anthropology/news.html
7. Artigen: http://www.artigen.com/
8. NewsHub: http://www.newshub.com/
9. NewsTracker : http://nt.excite.com/
10. TotalNews: http://www.totalnews.com/

Learning

There are a number of ways to learn on the net. One simple way is to subscribe to mailing lists or to monitor newsgroups on subjects that you want to learn more about. There are also a variety of short tutorials on the web that help you to learn about the Internet, the world wide web, and how to create web pages. Microsoft has tutorial pages for the Internet and the web (Internet Guide & Web Tutorial[1]). A nice set of tutorials on how to develop your own web resources is Webmonkey: A How To Guide for Web Developers[2].

There are only a few anthropology tutorials on the web. Kinship and Social Organization: An Online Tutorial[3] by Brian Schwimmer is one of the best for kinship. Dennis O'Neil at Palomar College is creating a series of Anthropology Tutorials[4] for different topics in bioanthropology and cultural anthropology. Richard Effland and Shereen Lerner at Mesa College have a wide variety of Anthropology Internet Activity Areas[5] for all fields of anthropology. At the World Lecture Hall[6] you can find online course materials for anthropology and archaeology courses (and for other subjects as well).

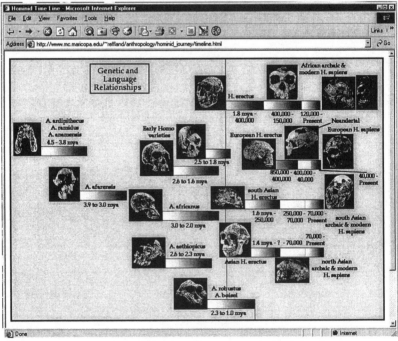

Hominid Time Life from Anthropology Internet Activity Areas

Online courses include longer, more formal sequences of material. Your university may offer distance education courses that you can take just as you would any other course. Online courses usually charge tuition. There are several consortia that provide information on distance education offerings for a number of universities. The largest include the Western Governors University[7], the Southern Regional Electronic Campus[8], and the National Universities Degree Consortium[9]. Before you sign up for a course check to see that the course is accredited by a recognized accreditation organization and that your university will accept transfer credit for the course.

Web Links

1. Internet Guide & Web Tutorial:
   http://www.microsoft.com/insider/internet/default.htm

2. Webmonkey: A How To Guide for Web Developers:
   http://www.hotwired.com/webmonkey/

3. Kinship and Social Organization: An Online Tutorial:
   http://www.umanitoba.ca/anthropology/kintitle.html

4. Anthropology Tutorials: http://anthro.palomar.edu/tutorials/

5. Anthropology Internet Activity Areas:
   http://www.mc.maricopa.edu/dept/d10/asb/activities.html

6. World Lecture Hall: http://www.utexas.edu/world/lecture/

7. Western Governors University: http://www.wgu.edu/

8. Southern Regional Electronic Campus:
   http://www.srec.sreb.org/http://www.electroniccampus.org/

9. National Universities Degree Consortium: http://www.nudc.org/

PART II.
RESEARCHING ANTHROPOLOGY ON THE WEB

Introduction

The web is a new research tool that can greatly assist your study of anthropology. All of anthropology is not on the web and coverage of many topics is patchy, but it is growing all the time. Any simple list of web sites is obsolete by the time it has been published. I have suggested a few places to get started with your research into various anthropological topics. With the search tools described in the previous section, you have what you need to find more and to find sites that appear after this book is printed.

As a student, you can use the web to supplement the material you are learning about anthropology from your textbook and from resources at the library. You can use the web to get the latest statistical data and news of discoveries made after your text was written. Use the web to place what you are learning in the classroom into a broader context that helps you to understand the world around you. You will be better prepared for class and will be able to participate in classroom discussions more effectively. The web can also help you to see the relevance of anthropology to other subjects that you are studying.

This part of the guide focuses on some specific areas of anthropology that you will be studying in class. For each area, the guide suggests some web sites that can help you to master the material in your text or can provide you with ideas for research papers or discussion topics. The areas listed here do not exhaust the topics that anthropologists study, but you should be able to use them to find information on topics that are not specifically covered here. The section on "Cultural Anthropology" introduces topics such as subsistence, social and political organization, religion, language, and economic development, among others. The section on "Physical Anthropology" includes information on non-human primates, human evolution, and human variation. The "Archaeology" section covers prehistory all over the world as well as historical archaeology and archaeological methods. The section on "Applied Anthropology" explores the areas of medical anthropology, the anthropology of business, forensic anthropology, and cultural resources management.

The section on "Applying Anthropology" shows you how to use the web to get information about field schools, volunteer opportunities and internships. Finally, "Careers in Anthropology" shows you how to use the web to find a job in anthropology.

Cultural Anthropology

Cultural anthropology is concerned with the diversity of human culture around the world. Cultural anthropologists are concerned with all aspects of human culture from subsistence and technology to social and political organization to religion and ritual. All of these topics have some coverage on the web and many of the general research tools described in the previous section will help you to find what you need.

There are many sites that classify and organize anthropology on the web. Three good places to start are the WWW Virtual Library: Anthropology[1] and Anthropology Resources on the Internet[2]. Together they span a great deal of information.

To understand more about cultural anthropology, you may want to visit some of the tutorials that are available. For instance, What is Culture?[3] created by Eric Miraglia, Richard Law, and Peg Collins at Washington State University has various definitions of the concept of culture. To learn about fieldwork, visit An Anthropologist in the Field[4], Laura Tamakoshi's site about her field work in New Guinea, or A Place Called Kaktovik[5], which describes Norman Chance's field experiences on the north slope of Alaska in 1958.

Ethnocentrism is the tendency to assume that your society and your way of doing things is the most sensible. Linda Steward illustrates the concept at her web site, Ethnocentrism[6] by discussing our perceptions of Saudi Women's clothing. The issues of cultural relativism are nicely summarized in Cultural Relativism and Universal Rights[7] by Carolyn Fluehr-Lobban in her article in *Active Voices: The Online Journal of Cultural Survival*.

The Ethnographic Atlas[8] at the University of Kent includes a brief description of 57 societies around the world. In addition, 186 societies have been classified according to 92 different variables. You can create tables between any pair of these variables. The variables include subsistence, post-marital residence, kinship terminology, type of housing, craft specialization and many more. You can quickly find out, for example, that the Aranda are the only group that have patrilineal and matrilineal moities and that patrilineal societies outnumber matrilineal ones by more than two to one.

For indices to web sites about particular regions, try the World Wide Web Virtual Library (WWW-VL): Regional Studies[9]. Particularly useful will be the following: Indigenous Studies[10], Aboriginal Studies[11], Circumpolar Peoples[12], American Indians[13], and Papua New Guinea[14]. Other good resources are the Center For World Indigenous Studies[15], NativeWeb[16], and First Nations dot Com - The Village of First Nations[17]. If your research involves Latin America, you should visit the Latin American Network Information Center - LANIC[18] web site.

Subsistence

Some of the best examples of foraging societies occupy arctic and subarctic environments. There are more imaginative web sites devoted to the people and the climate of the arctic than to any other biome. Be sure to visit the extensive Arctic Circle[19] at the University of Connecticut and the Arctic Studies Center[20] at the Smithsonian Institute National Museum of National History. The Canadian Museum of Civilizations has a nice online exhibit called Inuit 3D[21].

Journey to Other Worlds[22] is an Illinois State Museum exhibit on Siberian reindeer-herding cultures based on ethnographic materials from the Russian Museum of Ethnography. Reindeer People[23] is a virtual exhibit by Discovery Online on the Nenets reindeer herders, a people who are still living much as they did 500 years ago. The Lapps (now usually known as the Sámi) are well represented by pages on the Arctic Circle web site, The Sami of Far Northern Europe[24], and at An Introduction to the Sami People[25] by Boreale.

Ethnographic studies of the foraging societies of the Kalahari desert are the basis for much of what we know about the food-gathering way of life. You can find out more about the peoples of Botswana at Okavango Delta Peoples of Botswana[26] and at African San Communications[27].

Nomadic pastoralists are not as well covered on the web. The Bakhtiari have their own web site, Welcome to the Bakhtiari[28], where you can learn more about this pastoral society. You can read a bit more about them and see some impressive photos at The Iranian: Arts, Photography, Bakhtiaris[29].

Coverage for horticulturalists and agriculturalists on the web is also limited. Eggi's Village[30] describes life among the Minangkabau of Indonesia in a virtual exhibit at the University of Pennsylvania Museum. Rosemary Gianno created a page on the Semelai of Tasek Bera[31] for the Yale Peabody Museum. To learn about the Ashanti[32] Kingdom visit the web site being developed by Steve Garbrah. Clark Erickson at the University of Pennsylvania describes traditional raised field agriculture in the Amazon forest in Bolivia at <u>Ancient Raised Field Agriculture</u>[33].

Balancing food production with rising population requires new methods of cultivation and harvesting that do not lead to environmental degradation over time. Sustainable Development is another topic that is well covered on the web. To get started in your search, try the WWW Virtual Library: <u>Sustainable Agriculture</u>[34]. If your interest is in environmental impacts of development, try the WWW Virtual Library: <u>Ecology and Biodiversity</u>[35].

The <u>World Resources Institute (WRI)</u>[36], an independent center for policy research and technical assistance on global environmental and development issues, has many resources pertaining to the development and the preservation of the environment. A number of electronic publications are available online. You should also look at the <u>Sustainable Agriculture Page</u>[37]. The Center for International Earth Science Information Network (CIESIN) at Columbia University's <u>Agriculture Guide</u>[38] is a thematic guide that provides resources on agriculture and global environmental change. Particularly interesting is the section on <u>Indigenous Agriculture</u>[39] which has links to a number of interesting articles.

Social and Political Organization

Web resources devoted specifically to anthropological approaches to social and political organization are relatively rare. If you are looking for a particular society, try the sites mentioned in the introduction to this section. Michael Kearl's <u>A Sociological Tour Through Cyberspace</u>[40] does a nice job of addressing social and political topics from a sociologist's perspective. He combines topical summaries with links to web sites that can help you pursue topics in more detail.

Several web sites will help you learn kinship terminology, such as Brian Schwimmer's <u>Kinship and Social Organization: An Interactive Tutorial</u>[41]. Another nice tutorial has been created by Dennis O'Neil at Palomar College: <u>The Nature of Kinship</u>[42].

There are a few virtual ethnographies and articles on the web that provide information on particular societies. For example, <u>Descent, Clans, and Territorial Organization in the Tikar Chiefdom of Ngambe, Cameroon</u>[43] and <u>The Palace and Its Institutions in the Chiefdom of Ngambe</u>[44] by David Price describe the social and political organization of an African chiefdom. Carolyn Brown Heinz describes a Brahman caste in India in <u>The Mithila Brahmans: An Online Ethnography</u>[45]. <u>Peasant Social</u>

Worlds and Their Transformation[46] at the University of Manchester has a nice series of pages on the transformation of peasant societies in the twentieth century.

If you are studying contemporary American society, the U.S. Census department has statistics on Marital Status and Living Arrangements.[47] The page includes both current statistics and trends over the last 35 years. Another good source of information is the U.S. National Center for Health Statistics page called FASTATS[48], which provides a wide variety of health, social, and demographic statistics.

Religion

There are a number of sites that will help you research anthropological approaches to religion. The Anthropology of Religion Links and Lists[49] by the Anthropology of Religion Section of the American Anthropological Association has a comprehensive listing of web resources. The sociology of religion is also well covered on the web. The Sociology of Religion[50] is maintained by the Hartford Seminary. For the psychology of religion try Nielsen's Psychology of Religion Pages[51]. There are more general directories as well including the enormous Virtual Religion Index[52] maintained by the Department of Religion at Rutgers University. Also check the WWW Virtual Library: Facets of Religion[53].

To explore the major features of different religions try Religions, Faith Groups & Ethical Systems[54] which provides a brief synopsis of various religions. It should give you an adequate background to pursue more specialized resources. Another good resource is Ontario Consultants on Religious Tolerance[55]. To read religious texts online visit World Scripture[56] and Religious and Sacred Texts[57].

For information on traditional religions, there are a number of useful sites. You can learn about Shamanism[58], and receive answers to your most frequently asked questions. The Jon Frum Home Page[59] by Dennis Gaylor of the Centre for Reasonable Technology provides information about a particular cargo cult. Ancestors in Africa[60] is part of the Experience Rich Anthropology Project. It contains selected articles on ancestor worship in Africa, commentary, and case material on the Mambila.

For contemporary cults and sects try Alternative Religions[61] at About.com and the Watchman Fellowship's 2001 Index of Cults and Religions[62], which has a mammoth listing of cults and religious sects.

Belief in paranormal phenomena is widespread in contemporary society. Predictably there are many web sites (from all perspectives).

The following pages will give you some ideas about where to start. Steven Wagner's Paranormal Phenomena/The Unexplained[63] at About.com includes essays, news items, regular chats, and web links. Another extensive listing is Middletown Thrall Library ~ Links to the Paranormal and Beyond[64]. CSICOP On-line[65] is the Committee for the Scientific Investigation of Claims of the Paranormal. They publish the *Skeptical Inquirer* which uses scientific methods to debunk paranormal claims. Also worthwhile is Robert T. Carroll's The Skeptic's Refuge[66] which includes the The Skeptic's Dictionary[67] where you can research a wide variety of paranormal claims.

To explore the relationship between science and religion try the American Association for the Advancement of Sciences special program called AAAS Dialogue on Science, Ethics, and Religion[68] and the PBS web site called Faith and Reason[69].

Language and Linguistics

Anthropological linguistics is not well-represented on the web, but more general indexes to language and linguistics are. The World-Wide Web Virtual Library: Linguistics[70] is a good place to start searching for web sites that relate to linguistics. The page is sponsored by the Linguist List, an electronic conference, which also has a nice web site on linguistics, The LINGUIST List[71]. Tyler Chambers iLoveLanguages[72] contains links to over 1800 resources about language including dictionaries and language schools. You can find introductions, grammars, and dictionaries for many languages on the web. Michael Covington and Mark Rosenfelder answer Frequently Asked Questions About Linguistics[73] and provide information on how languages are related and whether English is a Creole.

How many languages are there? The Summer Institute for Linguistics catalogs over 6,700 languages at Ethnologue[74]. The pages are a bit dry, but they are the best place to find information on an obscure language (i.e. how many people speak it, where they live, and what other languages is it related to?). If Chinese (Mandarin), English, and Spanish are the first three languages in terms of population, what is the fourth?

Economic Development

Economic development and population growth are well covered on the web. Two good places to begin are the WWW-Virtual Libraries: Demography & Population Studies[75] and International Development[76].

The UN provides lots of information including statistics and charts on population, economic issues and agriculture. Try the Food and Agriculture Organization[77], the United Nations Statistics Division[78], and the United Nations Population Population Information Network POPIN[79]. Also look at the United Nations CyberSchoolBus[80]. It is geared for younger surfers, but the Resource Source[81] section has basic information about global trends and the member countries of the UN. The Population Reference Bureau[82] provides objective data on population trends in the U.S. and in the world.

The U.S government also provides a wealth of statistical information. For example, the US Global Change Research Information Office[83] lists educational resources related to global change. They also provide a number of online publications including *Consequences*[84]. The U.S. Census has data on world population at World Population Information[85].

If these don't have the data you need, Statistical Resources on the Web[86] from the University of Michigan is the best collection of links to statistical data on the web.

A consequence of population growth is that food production or food distribution may fail in one part of the world or another. The HungerWeb[87] explores the causes of, and solutions to, hunger. The web site is part of the Watson Insitute of International Studies at Brown University. Links to web resources relating to the ethical issues relating to world hunger can be found at Ethics Updates: World Hunger[88] by Lawrence Hinman at the University of San Diego. This web site is designed for students taking his Social Ethics course, but you can find web resources relating to hunger and its ethical implications.

Learn more about the concept of World Systems theory as developed by Fernand Braudel, Immanuel Wallerstein and others at The World Systems Archive[89], which provides many articles online. English versions of various Marxist publications are available at From Marx to Mao[90] and the Marxists Internet Archive[91]. You can also find internet versions of any of the classical economics literature online (e.g. Wealth of Nations[92] by Adam Smith and An Essay on the Principal of Population[93] Thomas Malthus).

Cultural Survival

Cultural Survival involves efforts by anthropologists to preserve cultural diversity around the world in the face of globalization. The Future of Tropical Rainforest Peoples web site, APFT Home Page[94], explores issues of biodiversity and cultural survival. Anthropologists at

APFT have prepared a report entitled <u>The Situation of Indigenous Peoples in Tropical Forests</u>[95] that describes the current population of tropical forest societies around the world and their prospects for the future. <u>Cultural Survival, Inc.</u>[96] has a web site with information on its efforts to preserve cultural diversity. Global human rights issues are the concern of <u>Amnesty International</u>[97] and <u>OneWorld Online</u>[98]. Also a good resource for web resources on human rights in the U.S. and the world is the <u>University of Minnesota Human Rights Library</u>[99].

<u>Institute for Global Communications</u>[100] was established to "bring Internet tools and online services to organizations and activists working on peace, economic and social justice, human rights, environmental protection, labor issues and conflict resolution."

Links to web resources concerning the ethical issues relating to multiculturalism can be found at <u>Ethics Updates: Literature on Race, Ethnicity, and Multiculturalism</u>[101] by Lawrence Hinman. <u>The Multicultural Pavilion at the University of Virginia</u>[102] has an extensive listing of web resources and activities to promote awareness of multiculturalism. Bill Henderson, an attorney in Ontario specializing in aboriginal rights, maintains a comprehensive list of <u>Links to Aboriginal Resources</u>[103].

Web Links

1. <u>WWW Virtual Library: Anthropology</u>: http://vlib.anthrotech.com/
2. <u>Anthropology Resources on the Internet</u>: http://home.worldnet.fr/~clist/Anthro/index.html
3. <u>What is Culture?</u>: http://www.wsu.edu:8001/vcwsu/commons/topics/culture/culture-index.html
4. <u>An Anthropologist in the Field</u>: http://www1.truman.edu/academics/ss/faculty/tamakoshil/
5. <u>A Place Called Kaktovik</u>: http://borealis.lib.uconn.edu/ArcticCircle/Museum/Anthropology/Kaktovik/arrival.html
6. <u>Ethnocentrism</u>: http://www.jcu.edu/communications/LSEWARD/ethno.htm
7. <u>Cultural Relativism and Universal Rights</u>: http://www.cs.org/publications/featuredarticles/1998/fluerhlobban.htm
8. <u>Ethnographic Atlas</u>: http://lucy.ukc.ac.uk/EthnoAtlas/ethno.html
9. <u>Regional Studies</u>: http://www.vlib.org/Regional.html

10. Indigenous Studies: http://www.cwis.org/wwwvl/indig-vl.html

11. Aboriginal Studies: http://www.ciolek.com/WWWVL-Aboriginal.html

12. Circumpolar Peoples: http://www.ldb.org/vl/cp/index.htm

13. American Indians: http://www.hanksville.org/NAresources/

14. Papua New Guinea: http://coombs.anu.edu.au/SpecialProj/PNG/Index.htm

15. Center For World Indigenous Studies: http://www.cwis.org/

16. NativeWeb: http://www.nativeweb.org/

17. First Nations dot Com - The Village of First Nations: http://www.firstnations.com/

18. Latin American Network Information Center - LANIC: http://www.lanic.utexas.edu/

19. Arctic Circle: http://arcticcircle.uconn.edu/

20. Arctic Studies Center: http://nmnhwww.si.edu/arctic/

21. Inuit 3D: http://www.civilization.ca/aborig/inuit3d/vmcinuit_e.html

22. Journey to Other Worlds: http://www.museum.state.il.us/exhibits/changing/journey/objects/index.html

23. Reindeer People: http://www.discovery.com/stories/nature/reindeer/reindeer.html

24. The Sami of Far Northern Europe: http://arcticcircle.uconn.edu/HistoryCulture/samiindex.html

25. An Introduction to the Sami People: http://www.itv.se/boreale/samieng.htm

26. Okavango Delta Peoples of Botswana: http://www.mindspring.com/~okavango/

27. African San Communications: http://kalaharipeoples.org/

28. Welcome to the Bakhtiari: http://www.bakhtiari.com/

29. The Iranian: Arts, Photography, Bakhtiaris: http://iranian.com/Arts/March98/Bakhtiari/

30. Eggi's Village: http://www.sas.upenn.edu/~psanday/eggi2.html

31. Semelai of Tasek Bera: http://www.peabody.yale.edu/exhibits/semelai/

32. Ashanti: http://www.ashanti.com.au/

33. Ancient Raised Field Agriculture: http://www.sas.upenn.edu/~cerickso/applied.html

34. Sustainable Agriculture: http://www.floridaplants.com/sustainable.htm

35. Ecology and Biodiversity: http://conbio.net/vl/

36. World Resources Institute (WRI): http://www.wri.org/

37. Sustainable Agriculture Page: http://www.wri.org/wri/sustag/

38. Agriculture Guide: http://www.ciesin.org/TG/AG/AG-home.html

39. Indigenous Agriculture: http://www.ciesin.org/TG/AG/iksys.html

40. A Sociological Tour Through Cyberspace: http://www.trinity.edu/~mkearl/

41. Kinship and Social Organization: An Interactive Tutorial: http://www.umanitoba.ca/anthropology/kintitle.html

42. The Nature of Kinship: http://daphne.palomar.edu/kinship/default.htm

43. Descent, Clans, and Territorial Organization in the Tikar Chiefdom of Ngambe, Cameroon: http://lucy.ukc.ac.uk/Rainforest/SML_files/Pricede/descent_TOC.html

44. The Palace and Its Institutions in the Chiefdom of Ngambe: http://lucy.ukc.ac.uk/Rainforest/SML_files/Pricech/chiefs_1.html

45. The Mithila Brahmans: An Online Ethnography: http://www.csuchico.edu/anth/mithila/

46. Peasant Social Worlds and Their Transformation: http://nt2.ec.man.ac.uk/multimedia/Default.htm

47. Marital Status and Living Arrangements: http://www.census.gov/population/www/socdemo/ms-la.html

48. FASTATS: http://www.cdc.gov/nchs/fastats/Default.htm

49. Anthropology of Religion Links and Lists: http://www.uwgb.edu/sar/links.htm

50. Sociology of Religion: http://hirr.hartsem.edu/sociology/sociology.html

51. Nielsen's Psychology of Religion Pages: http://www.psywww.com/psyrelig/index.htm

52. Virtual Religion Index: http://religion.rutgers.edu/vri/index.html

53. Facets of Religion: http://www.bcca.org/~cvoogt/Religion/

54. Religions, Faith Groups & Ethical Systems: http://www.religioustolerance.org/var_rel.htm

55. Ontario Consultants on Religious Tolerance: http://www.religioustolerance.org/

56. World Scripture: http://www.unification.net/ws/

56. World Scripture: http://www.unification.net/ws/

57. Religious and Sacred Texts: http://davidwiley.com/religion.html

58. Shamanism: http://deoxy.org/shaman.htm

59. Jon Frum Home Page: http://enzo.gen.nz/jonfrum/index.htm

60. Ancestors in Africa: http://lucy.ukc.ac.uk/Fdtl/Ancestors/

61. Alternative Religions: http://altreligion.about.com/

62. Watchman Fellowship's 2001 Index of Cults and Religions: http://www.watchman.org/indxmenu.htm

63. Paranormal Phenomena/The Unexplained: http://paranormal.about.com/

64. Middletown Thrall Library ~ Links to the Paranormal and Beyond: http://www.thrall.org/paranormal/

65. CSICOP On-line: http://www.csicop.org/

66. The Skeptic's Refuge: http://skepdic.com/refuge/sr.html

67. The Skeptic's Dictionary: http://skepdic.com/

68. AAAS Dialogue on Science, Ethics, and Religion: http://www.aaas.org/spp/dser/

69. Faith and Reason: http://www.pbs.org/faithandreason/

70. The World-Wide Web Virtual Library: Linguistics: http://www.emich.edu/~linguist/www-vl.html

71. The LINGUIST List: http://linguistlist.org/

72. iLoveLanguages: http://www.ilovelanguages.com/

73. Frequently Asked Questions About Linguistics: http://www.zompist.com/langfaq.html

74. Ethnologue: http://www.ethnologue.com/

75. Demography & Population Studies: http://demography.anu.edu.au/VirtualLibrary/

76. International Development: http://w3.acdi-cida.gc.ca/virtual.nsf/33313a7e6cfeb3a9852564040055d4ac/a8cbc39c015fe7c18525666d004e4830?OpenDocument

77. Food and Agriculture Organization: http://www.fao.org/

78. United Nations Statistics Division: http://www.un.org/Depts/unsd/statdiv.htm

79. POPIN: http://www.un.org/popin/

80. United Nations CyberSchoolBus: http://www.un.org/Pubs/CyberSchoolBus/index.html

81. Resource Source:
   http://www.un.org/Pubs/CyberSchoolBus/menureso.htm

82. Population Reference Bureau: http://www.prb.org/

83. US Global Change Research Information Office:
   http://www.gcrio.org/

84. *Consequences*:
   http://www.gcrio.org/CONSEQUENCES/introCON.html

85. World Population Information:
   http://www.census.gov/ipc/www/world.html

86. Statistical Resources on the Web:
   http://www.lib.umich.edu/govdocs/stats.html

87. The HungerWeb:
   http://www.brown.edu/Departments/World_Hunger_Program/

88. Ethics Updates: World Hunger:
   http://ethics.acusd.edu/world_hunger.html

89. The World Systems Archive:
   http://csf.colorado.edu/wsystems/wsarch.html

90. From Marx to Mao: http://www.marx2mao.org/

91. Marxists Internet Archive: http://www.marxists.org/

92. Wealth of Nations:
   http://www.econlib.org/library/Smith/smWN.html

93. An Essay on the Principal of Population:
   http://www.econlib.org/library/Malthus/malPop.html

94. APFT Home Page: http://lucy.ukc.ac.uk/Rainforest/page1g.html

95. The Situation of Indigneous Peoples in Tropical Forests:
   http://lucy.ukc.ac.uk/Sonja/RF/Ukpr/Report_t.htm

96. Cultural Survival, Inc.: http://www.cs.org/

97. Amnesty International: http://www.amnesty.org/

98. OneWorld Online: http://www.oneworld.net/

99. University of Minnesota Human Rights Library:
   http://www1.umn.edu/humanrts/

100. Institute for Global Communications: http://www.igc.org/igc/

101. Ethics Updates: Literature on Race, Ethnicity, and
   Multiculturalism: http://ethics.acusd.edu/race.html

102. The Multicultural Pavilion at the University of Virginia:
   http://curry.edschool.virginia.edu/go/multicultural/home.html

103. Links to Aboriginal Resources:
   http://www.bloorstreet.com/300block/aborl.htm

Physical Anthropology

The field of physical anthropology (or bioanthropology) includes the study of living and fossil non-human primates, human evolution, and human genetic and physical variability. The first two topics are well-covered on the web, but you may have to dig into bioscience and medical sites to find information about the third. Some general places to start your search are the sections on physical anthropology and human evolution at Biological Anthropology Web[1]. Also check Biological Anthropology Resources on the World Wide Web[2] by Karen Supak. The Anthropology Tutorials Menu[3] by Dennis O'Neil includes a number of good introductions to the various aspects of bioanthropology.

Non-Human Primates

The most comprehensive listing of web sites with information about primates is Ken Boschert's Primate Sites[4]. The Primate Info Net[5] at the Wisconsin Regional Primate Research Center provides numerous links to information about primates and the people studying them. Particularly useful is the About the Primates[6] section which has links to sites that list basic facts and describe primate anatomy, behavior, evolution, taxonomy, and folklore. Primate Photo Gallery[7] specializes in pictures of many different primate species. Currently, their coverage of lemurs is better than other taxa so it is the best place to discover the difference between the indri and the sifaka. See and hear chimpanzees, gorillas, and four species of monkeys at African Primates at Home[8], developed by M. K. Holder. The World Wildlife Fund has information about bonobos, chimpanzees, gorillas, and orangutans at Great Apes in the Wild[9]. The site also includes information on their current geographical distribution and threats to their survival. You can learn about the primary locations in Africa for studying apes at African Ape Study Sites[10] by Jim Moore at the University of California at San Diego.

You can find out about the current status and threats to bonobos (*Pan paniscus*) at Bonobo Protection Fund[11]. Bonobo Sex and Society[12] by Frans B. M. de Waal was originally published in 1995 in *Scientific American*. It describes his observations of bonobos that he believes challenge the assumptions about male supremacy in human evolution.

M. Nakamura tells you about chimpanzee (*Pan troglodytes*) research sites in The World of Chimpanzees[13]. The Chimpanzee and Human Communication Institute[14] at Central Washington University describes efforts to communicate with chimps. Emory University's Living Links web site has <u>Videos</u>[15] of chimpanzee conflict and food sharing. Finally you can learn about Jane Goodall at <u>Famous Faces</u>[16] by the National Geographic Society and <u>Jane Goodall's Wild Chimpanzees</u>[17] by PBS/Nature. <u>The Predatory Behavior and Ecology of Wild Chimpanzees</u>[18] by Craig Stanford considers what we can learn about our early ancestors from studying hunting by modern chimpanzees.

The Dian Fossey Fund has a page on <u>Mountain Gorilla Protection</u>[19] (*Gorilla gorilla*) and <u>The Gorilla Foundation</u>[20] also has a page on protecting gorillas. The PBS/Nature site has a virtual exhibit on efforts to communicate with a gorilla using sign language at <u>A Conversation With Koko</u>[21].

Orangutans (*Pongo pygmaeus*) are the only great ape that lives in southeast Asia rather than Africa. <u>Orang Utan</u>[22] by the Department of Tourism of Indonesia has pictures of orangutans and links to other pages. It also gives instructions on how to get to areas where you can observe orangutans. You can find out more about the leading authority on orangutans, <u>Birute Galdikas</u>[23]. <u>Orangutan Foundation International</u>[24] discusses efforts to protect orangutans from extinction. PBS/Nature has a virtual exhibit called <u>Orangutans: Just Hangin' On</u>[25], and the Discovery channel has a site describing efforts to save this endangered species, <u>Saving the Orangutans of Indonesia</u>[26].

Human Evolution

There are a number of good web sites to help you learn about genetics and evolution. One place to visit is <u>MendelWeb</u>[27] which has a number of nice resources, including an English translation of Mendel's paper describing his "Theory of Particulate Inheritance."

The best web site for information about evolution, creationism, and thoughtful discussion is <u>The Talk.Origins Archive</u>[28]. Read Chris Colby's <u>Introduction to Evolutionary Biology</u>[29] for a thorough introduction to the issues in evolutionary biology. <u>The Talk.Origins Archive: Must-Read FAQs</u>[30] will give you an excellent introduction to the various issues and debates. Another valuable reference is <u>Fossil Hominds</u>[31] by Jim Foley, which identifies the various fossil hominids and their characteristics. If you are having difficulty keeping track of all of the hominid species or you want more information than the text provides, this is the place to go.

<u>Science and Creationism</u>[32] by National Academy of Science offers a variety of resources about evolution and the nature of science. For the other side of the issue, there are a number of creationist web sites. One that takes direct aim at Talk.Origins (described above) is <u>The True.Origin</u>

Archive[33]. For several more examples of creationist web sites, look at the index at The Talk.Origins Archive: Other Web Sites[34].

The Long Foreground -Overview of Human Evolution[35] is a tutorial by Richard Law. There are three modules that will help you with this and subsequent chapters in the text: an Overview of Human Evolution, a Hominid Species Timeline, and Human Physical Characteristics. The Hunterian Museum at the University of Glasgow has a series of annotated slides on the web called the Guided Tour of Hominid Evolution[36]. Human Prehistory[37] by D. I. Loizos provides some nice illustrations of fossil hominids, stone tools, and paleolithic art. You might also want to explore Outpost: Human Origins[38] on the National Geographic web site, particularly the Interpretation Station.

You can view 3D images of primate and fossil hominid skulls at Human Evolution: The Fossil Evidence in 3D[39] by Phillip Walker and Edward Hagen at the University of California at Santa Barbara. You can view a time line to select a skull and then rotate it through 360 degrees in the horizontal plane. You will need the Shockwave plugin for your browser.

Human Variation

To learn more about molecular genetics visit Primer on Molecular Genetics[40] written by Dan Jacobson. You might also spend a little time at the The Gene School[41] where you can learn about the foundations and history of genetics. John Hockenberry has a series of audio programs, The DNA Files[42], that provide insight into modern genetics and ethical issues.

Every introductory course in anthropology or bioanthropology discusses the genetics of human blood types, lactose intolerance, and sickle cell anemia. You can learn more about blood types from the Blood Types Tutorial[43], part of the Biology Project at the University of Arizona. Lactose Intolerance[44] is discussed at this web site maintained by the National Institute of Diabetes and Digestive and Kidney Diseases of the National Institutes of Health. For questions about The Human Genome Project Information[45] the web site at the Oak Ridge National Laboratory has the answers. Visit the Sickle Cell Anemia Virtual Laboratory[46] to learn more about this genetically transmitted disease. Frank Browing, a reporter for the "Sounds Like Science" program on NPR did two programs in early 1999 on race. At the NPR web site, you can listen to Science and Race I[47], which discusses race and susceptibility to certain illnesses and Science and Race II[48] that explores the causes of some of these conditions.

Much of the controversy over race and IQ scores hinges on an assumption that a significant part of what we are measuring when we give IQ tests is inherited ability. One problem is that IQ scores have not remained constant over the last several years, but have steadily risen suggesting that substantial differences in IQ could be entirely the result of education and other cultural factors. Read Rising Scores on Intelligence Tests[49] in *American Scientist* by Ulric Neisser to learn the basic details, and then listen to the report from NPR by Michelle Trudeau (IQ tests steadily rising[50]). For information on what IQ is and what it has to do with succeeding in a complex, modern society such as our own read The Role of Intelligence in Modern Society[51] in *American Scientist* by Earl Hunt. Finally, look at How Heritability Misleads about Race[52] by Ned Block to better understand the term "heritability."

Web Links

1. Biological Anthropology Web: http://www.bioanth.org/
2. Biological Anthropology Resources on the World Wide Web: http://www.geocities.com/CapeCanaveral/Lab/9893/
3. Anthropology Tutorials Menu: http://anthro.palomar.edu/tutorials/physical.htm
4. Primate Sites: http://netvet.wustl.edu/primates.htm
5. Primate Info Net: http://www.primate.wisc.edu/pin/
6. About the Primates: http://www.primate.wisc.edu/pin/aboutp.html
7. Primate Photo Gallery: http://www.primates.com/
8. African Primates at Home: http://www.indiana.edu/~primate/primates.html
9. Great Apes in the Wild: http://www.panda.org/resources/publications/species/greatapes/
10. African Ape Study Sites: http://weber.ucsd.edu/~jmoore/apesites/
11. Bonobo Protection Fund: http://www.gsu.edu/~wwwbpf/
12. Bonobo Sex and Society: http://www.mc.maricopa.edu/anthro/origins/bonobos.html
13. The World of Chimpanzees: http://jinrui.zool.kyoto-u.ac.jp/ChimpHome/chimpanzeeE.html
14. Chimpanzee and Human Communication Institute: http://www.cwu.edu/~cwuchci/
15. Video: http://www.emory.edu/LIVING_LINKS/a/video.html

16. Famous Faces:
    http://www.nationalgeographic.com/faces/goodall/index.html

17. Jane Goodall's Wild Chimpanzees:
    http://www.pbs.org/wnet/nature/goodall/

18. The Predatory Behavior and Ecology of Wild Chimpanzees:
    http://www-rcf.usc.edu/~stanford/chimphunt.html

19. Mountain Gorilla Protection: http://www.informatics.org/gorilla/

20. The Gorilla Foundation: http://www.gorilla.org/

21. A Conversation With Koko:
    http://www.pbs.org/wnet/nature/koko/index.html

22. Orang Utan:
    http://www.tourismindonesia.com/index_orang_utan.html

23. Birute Galdikas:
    http://www.science.ca/scientists/scientistprofile.php?pID=7

24. Orangutan Foundation International:
    http://www.orangutan.org/home/home.php

25. Orangutans: Just Hangin' On:
    http://www.pbs.org/wnet/nature/orangutans/

26. Saving the Orangutans of Indonesia:
    http://www.discovery.com/stories/nature/orangs/orangs.html

27. MendelWeb: http://www.netspace.org/MendelWeb/

28. The Talk.Origins Archive: http://www.talkorigins.org/

29. Introduction to Evolutionary Biology:
    http://www.talkorigins.org/faqs/faq-intro-to-biology.html

30. The Talk.Origins Archive: Must-Read FAQs:
    http://www.talkorigins.org/origins/faqs-mustread.html

31. Fossil Hominds: http://www.talkorigins.org/faqs/homs/

32. Science and Creationism: http://www4.nas.edu/opus/evolve.nsf

33. The True.Origin Archive: http://www.trueorigin.org/

34. The Talk.Origins Archive: Other Web Sites:
    http://www.talkorigins.org/origins/other-links.html

35. Long Foreground -Overview of Human Evolution:
    http://www.wsu.edu:8001/vwsu/gened/learn-modules/top_longf
    or/overview/overvw1.html

36. Guided Tour of Hominid Evolution:
    http://www.hunterian.gla.ac.uk/museum/hominid/hominid.html

37. Human Prehistory: http://users.hol.gr/~dilos/prehis.htm

38. Outpost: Human Origins:
http://www.nationalgeographic.com/outpost/index.html

39. Human Evolution: The Fossil Evidence in 3D:
http://www.anth.ucsb.edu/projects/human/

40. Primer on Molecular Genetics:
http://www.genome.iastate.edu/edu/doe/

41. The Gene School: http://library.thinkquest.org/28599/

42. The DNA Files: http://www.dnafiles.org/

43. Blood Types Tutorial:
http://www.biology.arizona.edu/human_bio/problem_sets/
blood_types/Intro.html

44. Lactose Intolerance:
http://www.niddk.nih.gov/health/digest/pubs/lactose/lactose.ht
m

45. The Human Genome Project: http://www.ornl.gov/hgmis/

46. Sickle Cell Anemia Virtual Laboratory:
http://k14education.uams.edu/SickleCell/

47. Science and Race I:
http://www.npr.org/ramfiles/sls/19990102.sls.04.ram

48. Science and Race II:
http://www.npr.org/ramfiles/sls/19990102.sls.05.ram

49. Rising Scores on Intelligence Tests:
http://www.amsci.org/amsci/articles/97articles/neisser.html

50. IQ tests steadily rising:
http://www.npr.org/ramfiles/970917.atc.14.ram

51. The Role of Intelligence in Modern Society:
http://www.amsci.org/amsci/articles/95articles/Hunt.html

52. How Heritability Misleads about Race:
http://www.nyu.edu/gsas/dept/philo/faculty/block/papers/Heritab
ility.html

Archaeology

Of all the fields of anthropology, archaeology gets the most coverage on the web. Public interest in archaeology and the opportunity to transmit color images of ruins and artifacts makes archaeology well-suited to the web. You will find good general lists of links at Kris Hirst's About Archaeology[1] and at ArchNet[2], the WWW Virtual Library for archaeology. For lists relating to one kind of archaeology, try Underwater Archaeology[3]. Archaeology on the web can be divided into several broad areas. General prehistory sites for the Old World give good coverage to Europe but only sketchy coverage to Africa and Asia. Near Eastern and classical sites are well represented. North America and Latin America (especially Mesoamerica) have a number of good sites as well. Historical archaeology has limited coverage. The resources on archaeological methods also are somewhat limited, but are growing.

Old World Prehistory

The best place to begin your search for European sites is the WWW Virtual Library: Archaeological Resource Guide for Europe[4]. You can find sites by location or by time period, but the search engine is rather slow.

Neanderthals get lots of attention on the web. Chris Hawkins has created Neanderthal Heaven[5], "A Site Devoted to All Things Neanderthal." Not quite as serious as some of the other neanderthal sites, Hawkins includes basic information about the distribution, tools, morphology, and what happened to them. Kharlena Maria Ramanan has created a nice web site, Neandertals: A Cyber Perspective[6], with a great deal of information concerning their morphology, life ways, linguistic capacity, and ultimate fate. Another perspective on what happened to neanderthals is presented by Richard Klein in an essay, Behavioral and Biological Origins of Modern Humans[7].

Cave paintings are the most dramatic evidence of human culture during the Upper Paleolithic. The web has a number of sites that celebrate European Paleolithic sites. Probably the most dramatic is La Grotte de Lascaux[8] by the French Ministry of Culture and Communication. Lascaux is not the only cave in Europe with dramatic cave paintings. You should also visit the French Ministry of Culture and Communication's page on Chauvet Cave[9]. Tim Appenzeller explores the origins of Paleolithic art and the evidence for neanderthal art in a short article, Evolution or Revolution?[10] for *Science*. The Institute For Ice Age Studies[11] has a series of articles in their library by Randall White, an authority on paleolithic art.

To find out about the prehistory of Australia and the Pacific, visit Archaeology World[12]. The most famous site in the Pacific is described in a NOVA web site that complements a documentary video, Secrets of Easter Island[13].

Near East/Classical Archaeology

The best index to web resources on Mesopotamia and Egypt is Abzu: Guide to Resources for the Study of the Ancient Near East Available on the Internet[14].

There are two online tutorials on the origins of plant and animal domestication. One, The Domestication of Plants and Animals - the Agricultural Revolution[15], was developed by Richard Effland and the other, Agricultural Revolution[16] was developed by Richard Law. New excavations by Cambridge University at Çatalhöyük[17] in Turkey are allowing archaeologists to study the agriculture and sedentism as it developed 9,000 years ago, eventually leading to the development of cities. The web site describes a large-scale, interdisciplinary research program being conducted at the site and includes excavation diaries and progress reports.

European agriculturalists left their mark on the landscape in many ways. One of these was through the construction of tombs and other structures from large blocks of stone (megaliths). You can find out more about these sites at Stone Pages - A Guide to European Megaliths[18]. A nice photographic guide to megalithic sites in the British Isles is Megalithic Mysteries - A Photographic Guide[19]. If you need more information you can browse the list of sites that are part of The Stone Circle[20] Web ring. The most famous megalithic site is the stone circle at Stonehenge. The sites just mentioned have information on Stonehenge, but you will also find whole web sites devoted to this site and the bizarre theories that people have devised to explain it. Chris Whitcombe at Sweet Briar College has a nice summary of the site on his page Earth Mysteries: Stonehenge[21]. You should also visit The Complete Stonehenge[22] by Emily Mace, a student at Amherst University. The most famous inhabitant of this time was discovered in the Alps. Find out more about Ötzi, better known as the Iceman[23], at Discovery Online.

Richard Effland has created an online tutorial on the rise of civilizations, The Cultural Evolution of Civilizations[24] which will help you master the material in your text. The University of Michigan, Museum of Anthropology has a nice virtual exhibit describing Archaeological Research on the Deh Luran Plain, Southwestern Iran[25] that illustrates the chronological sequence of the area during the period when the first city states emerged.

As you might imagine, Ancient Egypt is very well represented on the web. The following list will get you started, but is not exhaustive. First visit the Canadian Museum of Civilization's site, Mysteries of Egypt[26] for an overview. Visit Katherine Mann's site, The Tomb of Tutankhamen[27] to find out more about the most famous Egyptian and then move on to the National Geographic Society's At the Tomb of Tutankhamen[28]. In Pyramids -- The Inside Story[29] NOVA lets you explore the Great Pyramid and learn about an archaeological excavation of one of the bakeries that provided food for the laborers. The site is a good complement to the NOVA video, *This Old Pyramid*. The Great Temple of Abu Simbel[30], includes a virtual tour of the temple built by Ramses II in the 13th century B.C. Tomb Tales[31] by Discovery Online describes recent discoveries in Egypt.

Shifting to the Roman Empire, Pompeii Forum Project[32] by the University of Virginia, describes interdisciplinary research project using remote sensing to discover more about the ancient city.

Mysterious Mummies of China[33] by NOVA has information about the Takla Makan mummies and "Mummies 101," describing how mummies are preserved. Desert Mummies[34] by Discovery Online also describes the Takla Makan mummies.

Indus Valley[35] includes information about the ancient Harappan Civilization, the Indus script (an untranslated language), and a 3D virtual model of the Harappa site.

Finally, Exploring Ancient World Cultures[36] is an extensive site featuring virtual explorations of several world cultures including the Near East, India, Egypt, Greece, Rome, Islam, and Europe.

New World Prehistory

There are two general indexes to North American Prehistory that are useful. One is Kevin Callahan's The Archaeology of North America[37] and the other is WebWeaver's North American Archaeology Links[38]. For regional coverage, the best introduction to southwestern archaeology is Southwestern Archaeology[39]. If you are interested in arctic prehistory, try Archaeology in Arctic North America[40].

The complex civilizations of Mesoamerica are also well-represented on the web. First visit the extensive index of resources at Mesoweb[41].

Another good index to Mesoamerican resources is <u>Ancient Meso-american Civilizations</u>[42] by Kevin L. Callahan.

Within Mesoamerica, the Maya are better represented than any other society. A good introduction to the Maya is available at the Canadian Museum of Civilization's <u>Mystery of the Maya</u>[43] site. The <u>Lords of Copan</u>[44] by the National Geographic Society will introduce you to this famous site in Honduras. You can take a virtual <u>Journey Through Tikal</u>[45] at this site by Studio 360. You can learn more about the Mayan calendar and writing system at <u>Rabbit In The Moon: Mayan Glyphs And Architecture</u>[46] by Nancy McNelly. <u>Virtual Palenque</u>[47] is a virtual tour of another famous Mayan site by QVision. <u>Lords of Copan: Exploring a Maya Necropolis</u>[48] and <u>Copan Update: Maya Tomb Ransacked</u>[49] (National Geographic Society) explores Mayan tombs in the great city of Copan. <u>Collapse: Why Do Civilizations Fail?</u>[50] by Annenberg/CPB complements the "Out of the Past" series and focuses on the fall of the Mayan city, Copan.

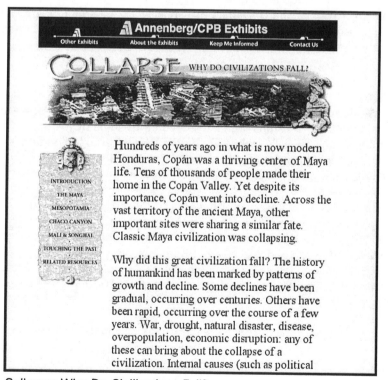

Collapse: Why Do Civilizations Fail?

The Valley of Mexico also receives good coverage on the web. The first city in Mesoamerica was Teotihuacan. The Saburo Sugiyama at Arizona State University has a Teotihuacan Home Page[51] that includes photos, maps, and QuickTime video tours of the city. Arizona State University also has the Templo Mayor Museum[52] site that has been developed by the Instituto Nacional de Antropología e História in Mexico to provide information about Tenochtitlan, the Mexica (Aztec) capital, now under Mexico City. Finally, The Tenochtitlan Web Site[53] presents a dramatic virtual world and tour of the capital city of the Aztecs.

There is less coverage of South America on the web and the available coverage focuses heavily on the frozen mummies. The National Geographic Society has Andes Expedition: Search for Inca Secrets[54] which includes a virtual autopsy and Ice Treasures of the Inca[55] about frozen mummies in the Andes. NOVA has Ice Mummies of the Inca[56] about the mummified remains at the summit of Sara Sara in the Andes. Discovery Online's site, Mummies in the Mist[57] also discribes the discoveries.

Santiago Uceda, Elías Mujica, and Ricardo Morales have a wonderful summary of the Moche culture at Huacas del Sol y La Luna[58]. You should also look at the University of Pennsylvania Museum of Archaeology and Anthropology's site, Stolen Moche Gold[59] which describes the return of stolen Moche artifacts.

Historical Archaeology

Web coverage of historical archaeology is not very good. However, you should be able to find web sites devoted to some of the more famous sites, especially if they are on the World Heritage List or are located on public lands. To find out about historical archaeology visit the The Society for Historical Archaeology[60] web site.

There are several web sites devoted to the Viking voyages to Greenland and Vinland. The Canadian Museum of Civilization has Canada Hall: The Norse[61] and the National Library of Canada has a nice article called, The Vikings: They Got Here First, But Why Didn't They Stay?[62] The Smithsonian Institution explores the colonization of Greenland and the discovery of the New World in A.D. 1000 in The Viking Millenium[63].

For information about recent excavations by the Jamestown Rediscovery Project, try Jamestown[64]. For a nice example of urban archaeology visit Five Points[65], which describes an excavation in New York City.

Archaeological Methods

You can find a bit about archaeological methods on the web, but you will have to dig. The best index is <u>Archaeology: An Introduction</u>[66] which is a companion web site to a text book on archaeological methods by Kevin Greene.

If you are trying to learn about archaeological dating methods, Mankato State University has summaries of many different dating techniques at <u>Dating Exhibit</u>[67]. There is also a nice summary of radiocarbon dating at <u>Radiocarbon WEB-info</u>[68], including the basis for the method and how dates are corrected and calibrated. For a good description of Bristlecone pines and their importance in calibrating radiocarbon dates, visit the <u>Ancient Bristlecone Pine</u>[69] page. <u>The Ultimate Tree-Ring Web Pages</u>[70] will tell you everything you need to know about dendrochronology and tree-ring dating. The page is maintained by Henri D. Grissino-Mayer.

There are a number of sites on the web that will help you learn about stone tools, what they look like, how they are used, and how to make them yourself. Start with the <u>Introduction to Stoneworking</u>[71] by Peter Hiscock . Then move on to the <u>Stone Age Reference Collection</u>[72] from the Institute of Archaeology, Art History and Numismatics in Oslo, Norway. To find other sites on stone tools, try \the lithics site\[73], maintained by Hugh Jarvis.

For information and links to sites showing how archaeologists analyze and interpret non-human bones in archaeological sites visit the <u>Zooarchaeology Home Page</u>[74] maintained by Frank J. Dirrigl Jr., Ph.D. and Barry W. Baker.

Fantastic or fringe archaeology concerns wild and unscientific claims that have been made about archaeological sites. There are a number of good sites that provide links and debunk the more bizarre claims. <u>The Wild Side of Geoarchaeology Page</u>[75] considers (and debunks) some fantastic claims made about archaeological sites that involve geology in one way or another (for example Atlantis) . Other good sources of information are <u>Martijn van Leusen's FRINGE ARCHAEOLOGY</u>[76] and <u>Doug's Archaeology Site: Skeptical Views of Fringe Archaeology</u>[77].

Web Links

1. About Archaeology:
   http://archaeology.about.com/science/archaeology/

2. ArchNet: http://archnet.asu.edu/archnet/

3. Underwater Archaeology: http://www.pophaus.com/underwater/

4. Archaeological Resource Guide for Europe:
   http://odur.let.rug.nl/arge/

5. Neanderthal Heaven:
   http://www.iinet.net.au/~chawkins/heaven.htm

6. Neandertals: A Cyber Perspective:
   http://thunder.indstate.edu/~ramanank/index.html

7. Behavioral and Biological Origins of Modern Humans:
   http://www.accessexcellence.org/BF/bf02/klein/index.html

8. La Grotte de Lascaux:
   http://www.culture.fr/culture/arcnat/lascaux/fr/index.html

9. Chauvet Cave:
   http://www.culture.gouv.fr/culture/arcnat/chauvet/en/

10. Evolution or Revolution?:
    http://www.sciencemag.org/cgi/content/full/282/5393/1451

11. The Institute For Ice Age Studies: http://insticeagestudies.com/

12. Archaeology World:
    http://arts.anu.edu.au/arcworld/arcworld.htm

13. Secrets of Easter Island: http://www.pbs.org/wgbh/nova/easter/

14. Abzu: Guide to Resources for the Study of the Ancient Near
    East Available on the Internet: http://www-
    oi.uchicago.edu/OI/DEPT/RA/ABZU/ABZU.HTML

15. The Domestication of Plants and Animals - the Agricultural
    Revolution:
    http://www.mc.maricopa.edu/dept/d10/asb/learning/lifeways/hg
    _ag/index.html

16. Agricultural Revolution:
    http://www.wsu.edu/gened/learn-modules/top_agrev/agrev-index
    .html

17. Çatalhöyük: http://catal.arch.cam.ac.uk/catal/catal.html

18. Stone Pages - A Guide to European Megaliths:
    http://www.stonepages.com/home.html

19. Megalithic Mysteries - A Photographic Guide:
    http://easyweb.easynet.co.uk/~aburnham/stones.htm

20. The Stone Circle:
    http://d.webring.com/webring?ring=stonecircle;list
21. Earth Mysteries: Stonehenge:
    http://witcombe.bcpw.sbc.edu/EMStonehenge.html
22. The Complete Stonehenge:
    http://www.amherst.edu/~ermace/sth/sth.html
23. Iceman:
    http://dsc.discovery.com/convergence/iceman/iceman.html
24. The Cultural Evolution of Civilizations:
    http://www.mc.maricopa.edu/~reffland/anthropology/lost_tribes
    /model_complex.html
25. Archaeological Research on the Deh Luran Plain, Southwestern
    Iran: http://www.umma.lsa.umich.edu/Oldworld/Deh_Luran/
    Deh_Luran.html
26. Mysteries of Egypt:
    http://www.civilization.ca/civil/egypt/egypt_e.html
27. The Tomb of Tutankhamen:
    http://www.inetsonic.com/kate/tut/index.html
28. At the Tomb of Tutankhamen:
    http://www.nationalgeographic.com/egypt/index.html
29. Pyramids -- The Inside Story:
    http://www.pbs.org/wgbh/nova/pyramid/
30. The Great Temple of Abu Simbel:
    http://www.ccer.ggl.ruu.nl/ccer/apps/Abu_Simbel/abu_simbel1.h
    tml
31. Tomb Tales:
    http://www.discovery.com/news/features/mummy/mummy.html
32. Pompeii:
    http://www.discovery.com/indep/newsfeatures/pompeii/
    pompeii.html
33. Mysterious Mummies of China:
    http://www.pbs.org/wgbh/nova/chinamum/
34. Desert Mummies:
    http://www.discovery.com/stories/history/desertmummies/
    desertmummies.html
35. Indus Valley: http://www.harappa.com/har/har0.html
36. Exploring Ancient World Cultures: http://eawc.evansville.edu/
37. The Archaeology of North America:
    http://www.geocities.com/Athens/Oracle/2596/

38. WebWeaver's North American Archaeology Links: http://www.mtsu.edu/~gdennis/nalinks.html

39. Southwestern Archaeology: http://www.swanet.org/

40. Archaeology in Arctic North America: http://watarts.uwaterloo.ca/ANTHRO/rwpark/ArcticArchStuff/ ArcticIntro.html

41. Mesoweb: http://www.mesoweb.com/

42. Ancient Mesoamerican Civilizations: http://www.angelfire.com/ca/humanorigins/index.html

43. Mystery of the Maya: http://www.civilization.ca/civil/maya/mminteng.html

44. Lords of Copan: http://www.nationalgeographic.com/copan/index-m.html

45. Journey Through Tikal: http://www.destination360.com/tikal.htm

46. Rabbit In The Moon: Mayan Glyphs And Architecture: http://www.halfmoon.org/

47. Virtual Palenque: http://www.virtualpalenque.com/

48. Lords of Copan: Exploring a Maya Necropolis: http://www.nationalgeographic.com/copan/index-m.html

49. Copan Update: Maya Tomb Ransacked: http://www.nationalgeographic.com/copan/index.html

50. Collapse: Why Do Civilizations Fail?: http://www.learner.org/exhibits/collapse/

51. Teotihuacan Home Page: http://archaeology.la.asu.edu/teo/index.htm

52. Templo Mayor Museum: http://archaeology.la.asu.edu/tm/index2.htm

53. The Tenochtitlan Web Site: http://www.cse.cuhk.edu.hk/~csc5460/mirror/handbook/

54. Andes Expedition: Search for Inca Secrets: http://www.nationalgeographic.com/andes/index.html

55. Ice Treasures of the Inca: http://www.nationalgeographic.com/mummy/index.html

56. Ice Mummies of the Inca: http://www.pbs.org/wgbh/nova/peru/

57. Mummies in the Mist: http://www.discovery.com/stories/history/mummies/mummies.ht ml

58. Huacas del Sol y La Luna: http://www.huacas.com/

59. Stolen Moche Gold:
    http://www.upenn.edu/museum/Exhibits/moche.html

60. The Society for Historical Archaeology: http://www.sha.org/

61. Canada Hall: The Norse:
    http://www.civilization.ca/hist/canp1/ca01eng.html

62. The Vikings: They Got Here First, But Why Didn't They Stay?:
    http://www.nlc-bnc.ca/2/16/h16-4223-e.html

63. The Viking Millenium:
    http://www.mnh.si.edu/arctic/features/viking/

64. Jamestown: http://www.apva.org/jr.html

65. Five Points: http://r2.gsa.gov/fivept/fphome.htm

66. Archaeology: An Introduction:
    http://www.staff.ncl.ac.uk/kevin.greene/wintro/

67. Dating Exhibit:
    http://kroeber.anthro.mankato.msus.edu/archaeology/dating/

68. Radiocarbon WEB-info: http://www.c14dating.com/

69. Ancient Bristlecone Pine:
    http://www.sonic.net/bristlecone/home.html

70. The Ultimate Tree-Ring Web Pages:
    http://web.utk.edu/~grissino/

71. Introduction to Stoneworking:
    http://arts.anu.edu.au/arcworld/resources/intro/intro.htm

72. Stone Age Reference Collection:
    http://www.hf.uio.no/iakn/roger/lithic/sarc.html

73. \the lithics site\:
    http://wings.buffalo.edu/academic/department/anthropology/Lithi
    cs/

74. Zooarchaeology Home Page: http://www.zooarchaeology.com/

75. The Wild Side of Geoarchaeology Page:
    http://www.intersurf.com/~chalcedony/wildside.shtml

76. Martijn van Leusen's FRINGE ARCHAEOLOGY:
    http://odur.let.rug.nl/arge/Themes/fringe.html

77. Doug's Archaeology Site: Skeptical Views of Fringe
    Archaeology: http://www.ramtops.demon.co.uk/

Applied Anthropology

Anthropology is applied in a wide variety of settings. Many anthropologists work with people in developing countries to facilitate economic development and to help reduce the cultural disruptions that can occur as a result of new technologies. Web sites and research tools that can help you with development issues are discussed in the Cultural Anthropology section of this guide. Some of the other ways that anthropologists can apply their knowledge of culture are described here. Medical Anthropology is the study of traditional medical practices and the best methods to introduce new medical practices in developing areas. The Anthropology of Business applies anthropological research techniques to the study of contemporary business. Forensic Anthropologists attempt to identify people from fragmentary skeletal remains. Finally, Cultural Resources Management involves the preservation of cultural heritage, particularly in those cases where development threatens a significant archaeological site.

Medical Anthropology

Medical anthropologists study health, health care, and illness in various societies to understand cultural differences in practices and perceptions. Medical anthropologists might study curing practices of remote tribal societies, the medicinal properties of tropical plants, the impact of introduced diseases on developing countries, or the best way to deliver information on nutrition and sanitary practices in a small rural community. The WWW Virtual Library for Anthropology is the best index to web resources pertaining to Medical Anthropology[1].

The Society for Medical Anthropology[2] is the primary professional organization for medical anthropology. The society publishes Medical Anthropology Quarterly: International Journal for the Analysis of Health[3]. The journal is not online, but you can look at the contents of previous issues. Anthropology & Medicine[4] also publishes research in medical anthropology. The journal web sites list the contents of recent issues so that you can develop an idea of the kinds of research conducted by medical anthropologists.

University of California at San Francisco, School of Medicine has a number of links relating to health and culture at Primary Care - Resource Links: Cross-Cultural[5]. The site provides links to better inform clinicians about how cultural differences affect medical care. The EthnoMed Home Page[6] at Harborview Medical Center, University of Washington provides cultural profiles and medical information for major refugee and immigrant groups in the Seattle area. <u>Folk Medicine in Hispanics in the Southwestern United States</u>[7] is a module in a course on Hispanic Health. It describes common maladies and their treatment.

<u>The African Background of Medical Science</u>[8] by Charles Finch, M.D. discusses medical practice in ancient Egypt and traditional medicine in central and west Africa. <u>To Cure and Protect: Sickness and Health in African Art</u>[9] is a virtual version of an exhibit at the National Museum of Health and Medicine. <u>Plains Indian Health: Traditional Indian Healing and Western Medicine</u>[10] is a virtual exhibit at the University of Pennsylvania Museum.

Traditional healers are sometimes called shaman. Visit <u>Shamanism</u>[11] to learn more about shaman as healers. Another nice web treatment of shamans is NOVA Online's <u>Warriors of the Amazon</u>[12].

Ethnobotany is the study of cultural differences in the uses of plants, including their use as food, construction materials, or medicines. <u>Ethnobotany</u>[13] at Access Excellence is a nice introduction and Steven King's article, <u>Medicines That Changed the World</u>[14] provides some nice examples.

<u>WHO/OMS: World Health Organization</u>[15] is the branch of the United Nations that is concerned with health issues. They provide information and statistics on the global distribution of disease and international efforts to eliminate it. <u>United Nations Children's Fund (UNICEF)</u>[16] has information about children's health.

In the U.S. the <u>Centers for Disease Control and Prevention</u>[17] monitors disease throughout the world and maintains statistics on morbidity and mortality. Their "Travelers' Health" section provides information about health risks and how to avoid them for any part of the world you are planning to visit.

Anthropology of Business

Anthropology brings several strengths to business. One is the participant-observer approach to research. This emphasizes looking at what people do, in addition to asking them what they do. Survey research can be affected by perceived power relationships within the corporate hierarchy so that people's responses are affected by what they think the goal of the research is. The participant-observer approach involves working with people over a longer period of time. This insider/outsider viewpoint often helps anthropologists gain understanding from a perspective different than that of labor, management, or survey researchers. The outcome of an anthropological investigation of a corporation often focuses on cultural factors that interfere with productivity or job satisfaction. These factors can severely impair performance in a large multicultural/multinational corporation.

CIO, a journal for information executives has an interesting idea. The next time you need a computer systems analyst, why not hire someone with training in anthropology? Read about this modest proposal at Think Tanks[18]. *Fast Company* has a story called Anthropologists Go Native In The Corporate Village[19] that gives examples of anthropologists working in corporate settings. *The New York Times* describes anthropologists working in Silicon Valley at Coming of Age in Silicon Valley: Anthropologists' High-Tech Niche[20]. Karen Stephenson is an anthropologist who consults with corporations to eliminate company inefficiency and red tape. You can read more about her research in Mapping the Invisible Workplace[21] in *CIO Enterprise Magazine*. Then visit her web site at NetForm[22].

Most corporate anthropology involves research at a single company (who is generally funding the research). The Silicon Valley Cultures Project[23] describes a ten year ethnographic study combining corporate and community anthropology to evaluate cultures living and working in the hi-tech communities of the Silicon Valley.

The Center for Ethnographic Research[24] conducts ethnographic research in many settings, including research on corporate culture and consumers. Their web page has links to information about a variety of their recent projects and a PowerPoint presentation on Ethnographic Methods for Business[25].

Ethnography in the marketplace involves observing shoppers to learn more about what factors encourage or discourage them from purchasing. NPR Morning Edition did a story called The Minds of Consumers[26] [RealAudio] that describes Paco Underhill's research into the subtle factors that go into people's decisions to buy products when they go shopping. The way products are displayed can determine whether shoppers even look at them, let alone browse, or decide to buy them. You can also read a chat transcript at ABC News with Underhill at Chat Transcript: Learning About The Science of Shopping with Paco Underhill[27]. Underhill has written a book called *Why We Buy: The Science of Shopping*. You can find reviews by USA Today, 'Science' of Shopping: Cater to Women[28], and Salon "Why We Buy"[29] on the web.

Cross-cultural business advice and cautionary tales are regularly in the news. Some recent articles include, Preparation Lays Foundation for

Business Success Overseas[30] in the *San Jose Business Journal* that focuses on the myths surrounding women in international business settings. You have probably already heard about the failure of GM's efforts to market the Nova in Mexico because they did not take into account a Spanish pun (No Va, Doesn't Go). It is repeated all over the web and in many anthropology and international business texts. As with so many great stories, it is an Urban Myth that you can read about at Urban Legends Reference Pages: Business (Don't Go Here)[31].

The Web of Culture[32] seeks to educate the World Wide Web community on the topic of effective cross-cultural communications in the global marketplace. It includes a number of useful reference materials including holidays around the world and the meaning of non-verbal gestures in many different countries. Despite the name, Cultural Factors in Business: An Incomplete Anthropological Bibliography[33], J. N. Hooker's annotated bibliography is a very useful resource.

Forensic Anthropology

Forensic Anthropology involves the study of fragmentary human remains in an effort to determine as much as possible about the individual. Forensic anthropologists attempt to determine the age, sex, height, race, and facial features of individuals from skeletal remains. They may be called to work with a few bones found in the woods, a mass grave containing the jumbled remains of many individuals, or a mass disaster such as a plane wreck or an earthquake.

The field of forensic anthropology was founded by Clyde Snow[34], William Maples[35], and Douglas Ubelaker. The Forensic Anthropologist[36] by Mann and Ubelaker is a good introduction to the field, and originally appeared in the FBI Law Enforcement Bulletin. The EMuseum at Minnesota State University at Mankato also has a good introduction at Forensic Anthropology[37].

For a more dramatic introduction, visit the ThinkQuest site on Forensic Science[38] which includes a page on Forensic Anthropology[39], complete with the theme from *Raiders of the Lost Ark*. Another ThinkQuest site Evidence: The True Witness[40] provides information about forensic science, including forensic anthropology. You can also take the role of KC Rodgers, ace detective to help locate a missing girl.

One aspect of forensic anthropology is the reconstruction of facial features from skeletal remains. Visit Welcome to the LSU FACES Lab[41] at Louisiana State University to learn more. There have been a number of movie treatments suggesting that Anastasia, daughter of the Tsar

Nicholas II survived the massacre that killed the rest of her family during the Russian Revolution. Read Deborah E. Allen's Case Study at <u>Anna or Anastasia?</u>[42] to see what forensic science tells us. The <u>Argentine Forensic Anthropology Team</u>[43] is world famous for its efforts to identify missing individuals and human rights violations. You can learn about a number of their cases at this web site.

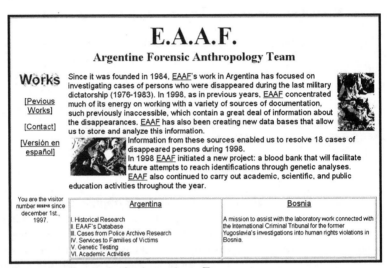

E.A.A.F.

Argentine Forensic Anthropology Team

Works

[Pevious Works]

[Contact]

[Versión en español]

You are the visitor number ■■■■■ since december 1st., 1997.

Since it was founded in 1984, <u>EAAF</u>'s work in Argentina has focused on investigating cases of persons who were disappeared during the last military dictatorship (1976-1983). In 1998, as in previous years, <u>EAAF</u> concentrated much of its energy on working with a variety of sources of documentation, such previously inaccessible, which contain a great deal of information about the disappearances. <u>EAAF</u> has also been creating new data bases that allow us to store and analyze this information.

Information from these sources enabled us to resolve 18 cases of disappeared persons during 1998.

In 1998 <u>EAAF</u> initiated a new project: a blood bank that will facilitate future attempts to reach identifications through genetic analyses.

<u>EAAF</u> also continued to carry out academic, scientific, and public education activities throughout the year.

Argentina	Bosnia
I. Historical Research II. EAAF's Database III. Cases from Police Archive Research IV. Services to Families of Victims V. Genetic Testing VI. Academic Activities	A mission to assist with the laboratory work connected with the International Criminal Tribunal for the former Yugoslavia's investigations into human rights violations in Bosnia.

Argentine Forensic Anthropology Team

A. Midori Albert at the University of North Carolina at Wilmington answers some frequently asked questions about <u>Forensic Anthropology</u>[44]. Another good introduction is Randy Skelton's <u>So You Want to Be a Forensic Anthropologist?</u>[45] The <u>Forensic Anthropology</u>[46] section of Osteo Interactive has a very nice introduction to the kinds of studies that forensic anthropologists conduct. Graduate programs in Forensic anthropology are also listed.

Cultural Resources Management

Cultural resources management involves the protection of important historic and prehistoric archaeological sites and artifacts. Many anthropologists who are trained in archaeology or bioanthropology are involved in cultural resources management in the United States. Outside the U.S., the term "heritage conservation" is more often used for similar activities.

The best overall index to cultural resources and historic preservation web resources is the <u>Preservation Internet Resources</u>[47]. The index is maintained by the National Center for Preservation Training and Technology. Also good is the CRM & Historic Preservation[48] section of ArchNet. The Heritage Preservation Services[49], a branch of the National Park Service provides information and links to laws and regulations pertaining to cultural resources management. The National Archaeological Database[50] has extensive bibliographic listings of cultural resources investigations. It also has information about compliance with the Native American Graves and Repatriation Act.

Almost any federal agency can be involved in cultural resources management. Any agency providing the land, funds, or permits to allow a project to proceed must consider the impact of the project on cultural resources. At the state level, the State Historic Preservation Officer (SHPO) consults with the federal agency involved. To find the one for your state check the list of SHPO's at National Conference of State Historic Preservation Officers[51] web site. Finally, the President's Advisory Council on Historic Preservation[52] can become involved at several stages in the process. Their web site has a number of informative pages on Section 106 of the National Historic Preservation Act.

Only sites listed on the National Register of Historic Places and sites that have been determined to be eligible for listing are protected. You can find out more about the National Register and the Keeper at National Register of Historic Places[53]. The National Park Service houses the National Register and Links to the Past (NPS)[54], a web site devoted to cultural resources management and historic preservation. The National Center for Preservation Training and Technology (NCPTT)[55] was created by the 1992 amendment to the National Historic Preservation Act. Visit their web site to learn more about their mission to provide training and support research in the preservation of buildings and artifacts.

The National Trust for Historic Preservation (NTHP)[56] was created to support the preservation of historic sites and structures around the country. The web site describes their activities and lists the most endangered historic sites.

The Register of Professional Archaeologists[57] is supported by the Society for American Archaeology[58], the Society for Historical Archaeology[59], and the Archaeological Institute of America[60]. The register is a listing of professional archaeologists who have a graduate degree in archaeology and who have agreed to adhere to a Code of Conduct and Standards of Research Performance. The American Cultural Resources Association[61] is a business organization for firms that conduct the cultural resources investigations required under federal and state laws. Some of these firms specialize in archaeological investigations while others provide a complete range of environmental investigations.

International Council on Monuments and Sites (ICOMOS)[62]. ICOMOS is an international non-governmental organization of professionals, dedicated to the conservation of the world's historic monuments and sites. The United Nations, Educational, Scientific, and Cultural Organization (UNESCO) includes the World Heritage Center[63] which maintains a World Heritage List of the most important historic (and prehistoric) sites. You can browse the list of sites at their web site. Preventing vandalism and pothunting worldwide is facilitated by international conventions designed to restrict the import of antiquities that have been illegally removed from their country of origin.

Vandalism and pothunting are problems in every country. Usually the motivation is the commercial value of the artifacts removed from federal lands or from one country to another. In the U.S., stone projectile points and prehistoric ceramic pottery are regularly found in antique shows and flea markets. When the materials come from private land and the excavators had the owner's permission, no laws have been violated (unless the artifacts are associated with human remains). However, if the artifacts come from federal or state land, they belong to the public rather than to any individual. In other countries, artifacts on private property can be considered cultural patrimony and their removal or export is illegal. A similar problem confronts nautical archaeology where the rights of salvage conflict with the need to carefully record shipwrecks during their excavation and the need to study intact artifact collections. The collection problem causes the most conflict since many salvage operations sell the ship's contents to fund their salvage operation. You will find many news stories on the web about pothunting and vandalism if you use one of the news search engines. For a couple of recent examples, look at the National Geographic page Copan Update: Maya Tomb Ransacked[64] on vandalism of Maya tombs in the city of Copan, or view Stolen Moche Gold[65] at the University of Pennsylvania Museum of Archaeology and Anthropology.

Web Links

1. Medical Anthropology:
   http://vlib.anthrotech.com/Specialized_Fields/Medical_Anthropology/
2. Society for Medical Anthropology:
   http://www.cudenver.edu/public/sma/
3. Medical Anthropology Quarterly: International Journal for the Analysis of Health:
   http://www.cudenver.edu//sma/medical_anthropology_quarterly.htm
4. Anthropology & Medicine:
   http://www.tandf.co.uk/journals/carfax/13648470.html

5. Primary Care - Resource Links: Cross-Cultural:
    http://medicine.ucsf.edu/resources/guidelines/culture.html

6. EthnoMed Home Page: http://ethnomed.org/

7. Folk Medicine in Hispanics in the Southwestern United States:
    http://www.rice.edu/projects/HispanicHealth/Courses/mod7/mod7.ht
    ml

8. The African Background of Medical Science:
    http://www.blackhealthnetwork.com/articles/article.asp?articleid=1
    717

9. To Cure and Protect: Sickness and Health in African Art:
    http://www.natmedmuse.afip.org/exhibits/past/cure/cure.html

10. Plains Indian Health: Traditional Indian Healing and Western
    Medicine:
    http://www.upenn.edu/museum/Exhibits/indianmedicine.html

11. Shamanism: http://deoxy.org/shaman.htm

12. Warriors of the Amazon:
    http://www.pbs.org/wgbh/nova/shaman/

13. Ethnobotany:
    http://www.accessexcellence.org/RC/Ethnobotany/

14. Medicines That Changed the World:
    http://www.accessexcellence.org/RC/Ethnobotany/page4.html

15. WHO/OMS: World Health Organization: http://www.who.org/

16. United Nations Children's Fund (UNICEF):
    http://www.unicef.org/

17. Centers for Disease Control and Prevention:
    http://www.cdc.gov/

18. Think Tanks: http://www.cio.com/archive/101596/dave.html

19. Anthropologists Go Native In The Corporate Village:
    http://www.fastcompany.com/online/05/anthro.html

20. Coming of Age in Silicon Valley: Anthropologists' High-Tech
    Niche:
    http://www.nytimes.com/library/tech/99/06/circuits/articles/10a
    nth.html

21. Mapping the Invisible Workplace:
    http://www.cio.com/archive/enterprise/071598_intellectual_cont
    ent.html

22. NetForm: http://www.netform.no/

23. The Silicon Valley Cultures Project:
    http://www.sjsu.edu/depts/anthropology/svcp/

24. Center for Ethnographic Research: http://iml.umkc.edu/cer/

25. Ethnographic Methods for Business:
http://iml.umkc.edu/cer/projects/consumers/ppeth/

26. The Minds of Consumers:
http://www.npr.org/ramfiles/me/19990722.me.05.ram

27. Chat Transcript: Learning About The Science of Shopping with Paco Underhill:
http://204.202.137.110/onair/DailyNews/chat_990511underhill.html

28. 'Science' of Shopping: Cater to Women:
http://www.usatoday.com/life/enter/books/book124.htm

29. "Why We Buy":
http://ww1.salon.com/books/review/1999/05/21/underhill/index.html

30. Preparation Lays Foundation for Business Success Overseas:
http://www.amcity.com/sanjose/stories/1999/04/12/focus2.html

31. Urban Legends Reference Pages: Business (Don't Go Here):
http://www.snopes2.com/business/misxlate/nova.htm

32. The Web of Culture: http://www.webofculture.com/

33. Cultural Factors in Business: An Incomplete Anthropological Bibliography: http://ba.gsia.cmu.edu/jnh/culture/refs.html

34. Clyde Snow:
http://www.anthro.mankato.msus.edu/information/biography/pqrst/ snow_clyde.html

35. William Maples:
http://www.anthro.mankato.msus.edu/information/biography/klmno/maples_william.html

36. The Forensic Anthropologist:
http://www.crimeandclues.com/forensicanthropologist.htm

37. Forensic Anthropology:
http://www.anthro.mankato.msus.edu/biology/forensics/index.shtml

38. Forensic Science:
http://library.thinkquest.org/17133/forensic.htm

39. Forensic Anthropology:
http://hyperion.advanced.org/17133/foranthro.htm

40. Evidence: The True Witness:
http://library.thinkquest.org/17049/gather/

41. Welcome to the LSU FACES Lab: http://www.ga.lsu.edu/faces/

42. Anna or Anastasia?:
http://ublib.buffalo.edu/libraries/projects/cases/Anna.html

43. Argentine Forensic Anthropology Team: http://www.eaaf.org.ar/

44. Forensic Anthropology:
http://www.uncwil.edu/people/albertm/forensic.htm

45. So You Want to Be a Forensic Anthropologist?:
http://www.anthro.umt.edu/studguid/forensic.htm

46. Forensic Anthropology:
http://medstat.med.utah.edu/kw/osteo/forensics/index.html

47. Preservation Internet Resources: http://www.ncptt.nps.gov/pir/

48. CRM & Historic Preservation:
http://archnet.uconn.edu/topical/crm/

49. Heritage Preservation Services: http://www2.cr.nps.gov/

50. National Archaeological Database:
http://www.cast.uark.edu/products/NADB/

51. National Conference of State Historic Preservation Officers:
http://www.sso.org/ncshpo/

52. Advisory Council on Historic Preservation:
http://www.achp.gov/

53. National Register of Historic Places: http://www.cr.nps.gov/nr/

54. Links to the Past (NPS): http://www.cr.nps.gov

55. National Center for Preservation Training and Technology
(NCPTT): http://www.ncptt.nps.gov/

56. National Trust for Historic Preservation (NTHP):
http://www.nthp.org/

57. Register of Professional Archaeologists: http://www.rpanet.org/

58. Society for American Archaeology: http://www.saa.org/

59. Society for Historical Archaeology: http://www.sha.org/

60. Archaeological Institute of America:
http://www.archaeological.org/

61. American Cultural Resources Association: http://www.acra-crm.org/

62. International Council on Monuments and Sites (ICOMOS):
http://www.icomos.org/

63. World Heritage Center:
http://www.unesco.org/whc/nwhc/pages/home/pages/
homepage.htm

64. Copan Update: Maya Tomb Ransacked:
    http://www.nationalgeographic.com/copan/index.html

65. Stolen Moche Gold:
    http://www.upenn.edu/museum/Exhibits/moche.html

Applying Anthropology

You will learn a great deal about anthropology in the classroom, but you will learn even more by applying anthropology. Anthropology students can develop practical skills and an appreciation for how the discipline of anthropology helps to orient their view of the world by participating in field schools, study abroad programs, working in an internship, and volunteering their time on research or development projects.

Field Schools

Before committing yourself to anthropology you might want to experience anthropological research in a field setting. Many colleges and universities have summer archaeological field schools and several have ethnographic field schools. For archaeological investigations look at the Archaeological Fieldwork Opportunities[1], Current Digs[2] at About.com, Archaeologic's Fieldwork Directory[3], and Archaeologyfieldwork.com[4], to find out about field schools and the need for excavation volunteers all over the world. In a field school you learn how to conduct archaeological investigations and how to process and analyze archaeological materials. You will probably get college course credit that you can apply toward your degree.

A few nonprofit foundations provide training in archaeological investigation for high school and college students as well as for teachers. The Center for American Archaeology[5] has educational programs for archaeological excavations centered near Kampsville, Illinois, involving Archaic sites, Hopewell mounds, and Mississippian villages. In Cortez, Colorado, Crow Canyon Archaeological Center[6] operates educational programs centered on prehistoric pueblo sites.

Other organizations look for volunteers or paying participants for archaeological and ethnographic research. The best known of these organizations, Earthwatch Institute[7], places participants with research projects in many different fields in many different parts of the world. Participants must pay for their expenses and a share of the expedition's research costs, but it can be a good way to find out if the field is really for you. A similar program is offered by the University of California Research Expeditions Program[8]. The goal of these programs is participation in ongoing research rather than education or training in a broad range of field skills, but they still offer excellent learning experiences.

Crow Canyon Archaeological Center

If you cannot afford the options above, you can volunteer your assistance to a USDA Forest Service project through <u>Passport in Time</u>[9]. These are archaeological and historical projects in National Forests around the country that are directed by Forest Service staff to preserve sites, recover data, or document collections. You pay for transportation and your room and board, but there are no other fees.

Once you have some field experience, you may be able to get a paid position on a cultural resources investigation. These projects involve archaeological and historical sites that are threatened by some form of development. Some of these investigations are conducted by research units within colleges and universities. Most of them are conducted by private organizations that specialize in archaeological investigations or in a broad range of environmental services (cultural resources investigations are governed by the same laws as Environmental Impact studies). Finding these positions can be challenging. First read <u>Summer Jobs</u>[10] on the American Cultural Resource Association web site and <u>Getting Your First Job in Cultural Resources Management: A Practical Guide for Students</u>[11] from the Society for American Archaeology Bulletin. Kris Hirst has a list of companies that regularly hire archaeological field technicians at <u>Field Assistant Contacts - Archaeology</u>[12].

Study Abroad

Your university probably has an office to help students find study abroad opportunities. Study Abroad programs fall into two broad categories. The first allows you to attend a university outside the U.S. and take courses in the local language. These programs typically place individual students. You will learn about the culture and language by being immersed in it. There is no better way to learn about another culture or to master a second (or third) language. Other programs involve groups of students (often from the same university) who travel together to learn about another culture. Language instruction is often part of the program. These programs are valuable, but since you can depend on other students (and faculty), you will probably be somewhat insulated from the host culture. First find out what kinds of Study Abroad programs your university is operating. On the web visit the web pages of the Council on International Educational Exchange[13] and AFS Intercultural Programs, Inc.[14] to find out about national Study Abroad programs. You can also check the WWW Virtual Library: Anthropology: Education/Study_Abroad[15] for a number of links to several Study Abroad programs.

Internships

Internship programs provide students with opportunities to learn by working with professionals. Internships can be used to train prospective employees or to provide a variety of job skills that have broad applicability. Good internship programs combine work and educational opportunities so that the intern is not just a poorly paid (or unpaid) employee. In addition to the guide, you will find an Advisor's corner and (soon) Case Studies. Another good site is the National Association for the Practice of Anthropology's NAPA Mentor Program[16] for internship advice.

Several branches of the federal government operate internship programs including the National Park Service. See their National Park Service: Employment Information[17] page for internship information. Also check the Center for Museum Studies[18] at the Smithsonian Institution. The State Department has a number of internships listed at US State Department - Services - Internships[19]. The Library of Congress has a Congress Junior Fellows Program[20] and the Volunteer Opportunities[21] with the Congressional Research Service.

International organizations also offer internship opportunities. If you are interested in international development, visit The World Bank - Young Professionals Program[22] or the United Nations Development Programme (UNDP) Internship Programme[23].

For internship opportunities in environment and resource conservation, check Volunteer, Internship, Employment[24] by the Student Conservation Association, Inc. For museum internships see the Internship Database--Museum Resource Board[25].

Rising Star Internships[26] maintains a listing of internships in a wide variety of areas. Try searching under several related categories if the one you are interested in is missing. Another good source is Idealist[27], the global clearinghouse of nonprofit and volunteering resources.

Don't be too disappointed if you don't find anything in these sites that seems just right for you. None of these resources is complete. You should also see if your university has listings of internships with organizations or agencies that are not listed on the web.

Volunteering

By volunteering your time, you receive the satisfaction of applying anthropology and learning marketable job skills. Volunteer programs range from weekends to several years in duration. You don't have to go far to find volunteer opportunities. Your local museum could probably use your help. Various social service agencies in your town such as food banks, shelters, literacy programs, and so on probably welcome volunteers.

If you want to volunteer for programs that are not available locally, you can get some help from the web. The Passport in Time[28] program operated by the USDA Forest Service uses volunteers to excavate archaeological sites, clean and catalog artifacts, inventory historical materials, and other activities. The web site lists when and where they need help and what the living conditions are like there. Volunteer America[29] is similar, but it lists volunteer opportunities on public lands all across the country. Another good source is Idealist[30], the global clearinghouse of nonprofit and volunteering resources which includes both volunteer and internship opportunities.

The United Nations needs lots of volunteers. Visit United Nations Volunteers[31] to find out what kinds of skills they are looking for and where those skills are needed.

If you are interested in environmental issues or cultural survival, look at the Volunteer, Internship, Employment[32] page at the Student Conservation Association[33] web site. You should check the Volunteer Information[34] page on the Rainforest Action Network web site as well.

If you are ready to volunteer for more than a few weeks, you should consider one of the two national agencies that place volunteers in longer term positions. If you want to stay close to home (or at least in the U.S.) visit The Corporation for National Service: AmeriCorps![35] web site. You can help fund your college education with AmeriCorps, but you can also work with them after college. If you want to travel far away, visit the Peace Corps: The Toughest Job You'll Ever Love![36] web site. While working for the Peace Corps, you will learn about another culture and probably master another language as well.

Web Links

1. Archaeological Fieldwork Opportunities: http://www.cincpac.com/afos/testpit.html

2. Current Digs: http://archaeology.about.com/cs/currentdigs/

3. Fieldwork Directory: http://archaeologic.com/fieldwork_directory.htm

4. Archaeologyfieldwork.com: http://archaeologyfieldwork.com/

5. Center for American Archaeology: http://www.caa-archeology.org/

6. Crow Canyon Archaeological Center: http://www.crowcanyon.org/

7. Earthwatch Institute: http://www.earthwatch.org/

8. University of California Research Expeditions Program: http://urep.ucdavis.edu/

9. Passport in Time: http://www.passportintime.com/

10. Summer Jobs: http://www.acra-crm.org/summerjobs.html

11. Getting Your First Job in Cultural Resources Management: A Practical Guide for Students: http://www.saa.org/publications/saabulletin/15-2/SAA7.html

12. Field Assistant Contacts - Archaeology: http://archaeology.about.com/science/archaeology/blcontact.htm

13. Council on International Educational Exchange: http://www.ciee.org/index.htm

14. AFS Intercultural Programs, Inc.: http://www.afs.org/

15. WWW Virtual Library: Anthropology: Education/Study_Abroad: http://vlib.anthrotech.com/Education/Study_Abroad/

16. NAPA Mentor Program: http://www.policycenter.com/policycenter/napa/mentormatch/napindex.htm

17. National Park Service: Employment Information: http://www.nps.gov/personnel/

18. Center for Museum Studies: http://www.si.edu/cms/

19. US State Department - Services - Internships: http://www.state.gov/www/careers/rinterncontents.html

20. Congress Junior Fellows Program: http://lcweb.loc.gov/rr/jrfell/

21. Volunteer Opportunities: http://www.loc.gov/crsinfo/volunteer/

22. The World Bank - Young Professionals Program: http://wbln0018.worldbank.org/hrs/hrs_www.nsf/key/ypp

23. United Nations Development Programme (UNDP) Internship Programme: http://www.undp.org/toppages/undpjobs/Interns/intern.htm

24. Volunteer, Internship, Employment: http://www.sca-inc.org/vol/vol.htm

25. Internship Database--Museum Resource Board: http://www.museumwork.com/internships.html

26. Rising Star Internships: http://www.rsinternships.com/

27. Idealist: http://www.idealist.org/

28. Passport in Time: http://www.passportintime.com/

29. Volunteer America: http://www.volunteeramerica.net/

30. Idealist: http://www.idealist.org/

31. United Nations Volunteers: http://www.unv.org/

32. Volunteer, Internship, Employment: http://www.sca-inc.org/vol/vol.htm

33. Student Conservation Association: http://www.sca-inc.org/

34. Volunteer Information: http://www.ran.org/what_you/volunteer_info/

35. The Corporation for National Service: AmeriCorps!: http://www.americorps.org/

36. Peace Corps: The Toughest Job You'll Ever Love!: http://www.peacecorps.gov/

Careers in Anthropology

If you like to study anthropology, but you are not sure if you can make it into a career, the web can help. You could major in anthropology and plan to enter graduate school to work toward an M.A. or a Ph.D. You could major in anthropology and plan to enter professional school (e.g. law or medicine). If you plan to work in international business, anthropology can give you a global perspective. You might minor in anthropology to combine the holistic approach to human societies with a more technical field such as engineering or agriculture. Anthropologists can be found in many professions. Their understanding of and sensitivity to cultural differences makes them valuable in a world where nation states are ethnically diverse. As part of your academic training as an anthropologist, you should try to apply your anthropological training in a summer field school, an internship, a study abroad program, or as a volunteer.

Anthropology Jobs

Most of the professional anthropological organizations have career guides on the web that describe how to become a professional anthropologist. They often include information about how to combine anthropology with other fields to improve your strengths in the job market. Careers in Anthropology[1] is a good general guide available from the American Anthropological Association. It is particularly good if you are planning to attend graduate school to become a professional anthropologist. Anthropologists at Work[2], prepared by the National Association for the Practice of Anthropology answers your questions about how to use anthropology in the workplace (they also have a video available). They also have a web site called NAPA Mentor Program[3] that provides career information and advice.

Other good sites include Careers in Anthropology: Where the Jobs Are[4] at Northern Kentucky University. It provides an extensive listing of jobs for anthropologists (particularly in Kentucky, but it will give you ideas about who to contact in your state). Also check Careers in Anthropology[5] at Indiana University/Purdue University, Indianapolis. The Princeton Review: Careers[6] has entries for anthropologist, archaeologist, and curator (you will have to register to research careers, but registration is free). The Bureau of Labor Statistics also has a listing for Social Scientists[7], which will let you know what the federal government is looking for when it comes to anthropology. Merry Bruns, at the Center for Anthropology and Science Communications, gives advice on combining anthropology and communications in CASC-For Anthropology Students[8].

Other career guides specialize in particular kinds of anthropologists. Careers in Archaeology[9] from the Society for American Archaeology (SAA) describes the training required to become a professional archaeologist and Careers in Historical Archaeology[10] by the Society of Historical Archaeologists (SHA) discusses historical archaeology (including underwater archaeology). More information about archaeology is available from Frequently Asked Questions About A Career in Archaeology in the U.S.[11] at the Illinois State Museum web site. Another good resource is Getting Your First Job in Cultural Resources Management: A Practical Guide for Students[12] from the *SAA Bulletin*. Finally, look at the National Park Service page: NPS Essential Competencies: Archeologist[13].

Careers in Physical Anthropology[14] is available from the American Association of Physical Anthropologists (AAPA) for those interested in pursuing the areas of bioanthropology, human evolution, primate ethology, human variability and related fields. A version of that brochure with hyperlinks is also available at BioAnthro Careers[15] at the University of California at San Diego.

Museum Careers[16] by the American Association of Museums lists information about museum careers. Another good resource, Museum Job Resources Online[17] provides advice on positions and internships in museums.

Finding Anthropology Jobs

Three good places to begin your search for anthropology jobs are WWW Virtual Library: Anthropology: Job_Opportunities[18], Jobs in Anthropology[19] (by Alexander Christensen), and Employment and Job Hunting[20] (by Kris Hirst). They provide links to sites that have job listings. If you want to learn more about the job market for anthropologists with graduate degrees, check the listings at AAA Job Database[21] at the American Anthropological Associations Web site. This is the most complete listing of academic positions for anthropologists.

For jobs in archaeology, including cultural resources management, check the Society for American Archaeology SAAweb - Job Announcements[22] and the Society for Historical Archaeology Employment Opportunities[23]. Primate-Jobs[24] on the Primate Info Net lists jobs in primatology. Applied anthropology positions are posted on the Society for Applied Anthropology SfAA Job Bulletin[25].

Many kinds of anthropologists find employment within the federal government. A number of federal agencies have their own job pages which may include advice for job seekers as well as job listings. For example, visit the Department of State Recruitment Site[26], the U. S. Department of Agriculture's Federal Employment in the USDA Forest Service[27], or the National Park Service NPS Employment Information[28]. USAJOBS[29] by the United States Office Of Personnel Management is the most complete listing of federal positions. Local government jobs are usually posted on agency web pages. There is one national index called GovtJob.Net[30] by the Local Government Institute.

Museum positions are listed in Museum Resource Board[31] which maintains a jobs database and a resume database. Museum Employment Resource Center[32] lists jobs in museums, cultural resources, and historic preservation. Job listings for the Smithsonian Institution in Washington, D. C. are posted at Job Vacancies[33]. Also check Global Museum 2000[34] which is located in New Zealand, but lists jobs in many different countries, including the U.S. You might also check OpportunityNOCs[35] (Nonprofit Organization Classifieds) or Nonprofit Jobs[36] by Philanthropy News Network for jobs with nonprofit organizations.

Finding Other Jobs

Once you are ready to start looking for a job, your first stop should be to contact your college placement office. They will provide services for listing your resume, contacting prospective employers, and arranging interviews. The web can also help you find job opportunities. There are many resources on the web that can help you post your resume and look for jobs. Many of these sites also provide tips on how to prepare your resume, and what to do before, during and after a job interview. While they are not specifically related to anthropology, they can still be useful:

4. America's Career InfoNet[37] is a partnership between the US Department of Labor and state operated public employment services. It includes America's Career InfoNet, America's Job Bank, and America's Learning Exchange.

5. CareerBuilder[38] is a private service of Career Builder, Inc. You create an agent to search their listings for jobs that you are interested in and they notify you by email of available opportunities. There is also a section on Managing Your Career.

6. The Employment Guide's CareerWeb[39] lists professional, technical, and managerial positions and allows you to post your resume. It also includes a variety of career resources.

7. FlipDog.com[40] combines listings from a wide variety of sources on their site and provides search capabilities.

8. The Monster Board[41] - has listings for thousands of jobs worldwide.

9. USAJOBS[42] by the United States Office Of Personnel Management is the most complete listing of federal positions.

Web Links

1. Careers in Anthropology: http://www.aaanet.org/careers.htm

2. Anthropologists at Work: http://anthap.oakland.edu/napafaq.htm

3. NAPA Mentor Program: http://www.policycenter.com/policycenter/napa/mentormatch/napindex.htm

4. Careers in Anthropology: Where the Jobs Are: http://www.nku.edu/~anthro/careers.html

5. Careers in Anthropology: http://www.iupui.edu/it/anthropo/careers.htm

6. The Princeton Review: Careers: http://www.review.com/Career/

7. Social Scientists: http://stats.bls.gov/oco/ocos054.htm

8. CASC-For Anthropology Students: http://www.sciencesitescom.com/CASC/student.html

9. Careers in Archaeology: http://www.saa.org/Careers/index.html

10. Careers in Historical Archaeology: http://www.sha.org/sha_cbro.htm

11. Frequently Asked Questions About A Career in Archaeology in the U.S.: http://www.museum.state.il.us/ismdepts/anthro/dlcfaq.html

12. Getting Your First Job in Cultural Resources Management: A Practical Guide for Students: http://www.saa.org/publications/saabulletin/15-2/SAA7.html

13. NPS Essential Competencies: Archeologist: http://www.nps.gov/training/npsonly/RSC/archeolo.htm

14. Careers in Physical Anthropology: http://physanth.org/careers/

15. BioAnthro Careers:
http://weber.ucsd.edu/~jmoore/bioanthro/Careers.html

16. Museum Careers: http://www.aam-us.org/infocenter/info03.htm

17. Museum Job Resources Online:
http://www.algonquinc.on.ca/museum/jobres/

18. WWW Virtual Library: Anthropology: Job_Opportunities:
http://vlib.anthrotech.com/Job_Opportunities/

19. Jobs in Anthropology:
http://anthropology.about.com/science/anthropology/msubjobs.h
tm

20. Employment and Job Hunting:
http://archaeology.about.com/science/archaeology/msubjobs.ht
m

21. Careers/Placement: http://aaanet.jobcontrolcenter.com/

22. SAAweb - Job Announcements:
http://www.saa.org/Careers/job-listing.html

23. Employment Opportunities: http://www.sha.org/nl-emp.htm

24. Primate-Jobs: http://www.primate.wisc.edu/pin/jobs/

25. SfAA Job Bullletin: http://www.sfaa.net/sfaajobs.html

26. Department of State Recruitment Site:
http://www.state.gov/m/dghr/hr/

27. Federal Employment in the USDA Forest Service:
http://www.fs.fed.us/people/employ/

28. NPS Employment Information: http://www.nps.gov/personnel/

29. USAJOBS: http://www.usajobs.opm.gov/

30. GovtJob.Net: http://www.govtjob.net/

31. Museum Resource Board: http://www.museumwork.com/

32. Museum Employment Resource Center: http://www.museum-employment.com/

33. Job Vacancies:
http://www.sihr.si.edu/vacancy/vacancy.cfm?close=close,mpan
um

34. Global Museum 2000: http://www.globalmuseum.org/

35. OpportunityNOCs: http://www.opportunitynocs.org/

36. Nonprofit Jobs: http://pnnonline.org/jobs/

37. America's Career InfoNet: http://www.acinet.org/acinet/

38. CareerBuilder: http://www.careerbuilder.com/

39. The Employment Guide's CareerWeb: http://www.cweb.com/

40. FlipDog.com: http://www.flipdog.com/home.html
41. The Monster Board: http://www.monster.com/
42. USAJOBS: http://www.usajobs.opm.gov/

Conclusion

It should be clear that the number of ways to incorporate the web into the study of anthropology is virtually unlimited. Providing you with a better context for topics raised in class or in your textbook is one of the easiest ways to use the web. Using the web to locate factual information can often provide results more quickly than traditional bound reference works. The web can deepen your understanding of anthropology and it can help illustrate the people, places, and things that anthropologists study. It can make you more effective in the library and can provide you with access to information that is not locally available. In short, the web can enrich your learning process.

GLOSSARY

Archie. A method of searching for programs on the Internet before the widespread availability of the web.

bandwidth. A measure of how fast data can be transmitted from one point to another in bits per second.

bookmark. A method of recording the address of a web site using your browser so that you can return to it without typing in the address.

browser. The software that interprets the formatting and programing codes that are contained in web pages. Browsers display web pages so that you can read them. They also transmit your commands back to the web site.

cookie. A small file on your computer that contains information that can be transmitted to a web site when you visit it. Cookies allow web sites to shop for products (they keep track of your shopping cart) and they allow you to customize web pages so that the content you want is there whenever you return.

domain name. Domain names are used to locate computers on the Internet. Minimally domain names consist of a name and a suffix. The suffix is usually .edu, .com, .net, .org, or .gov in the United States, but each country also has its own suffix (for example, the United Kingdom is .uk).

electronic bulletin board. Electronic bulletin boards allow visitors to post messages that can be read by others. The advantage of a bulletin board is that the messages are not distributed as email messages so they do not all end up in your mailbox whether you are interested in them or not. The disadvantage is that the messages drop off the board after a few days or weeks so that you can miss messages if you do not check the board regularly. The biggest collection of bulletin boards is **usenet** (see below).

Email. Short for electronic mail, email consists of text messages that are sent from one person to another person. The message waits at the recipient's mailbox until it is discarded by the recipient.

Frequently Asked Questions (FAQ). Frequently Asked Questions are collections of common questions and their answers that have been written by people all over the world. They are not limited to topics concerning the Internet or computers. Originally these documents were distributed by usenet, but now they typically reside on a web site. There are FAQs on almost any topic you can imagine.

Gopher. A precursor of the **World Wide Web** (see below). Gopher distributed text files that could be displayed by software programs (called gopher clients). Image and sound files could also be retrieved, but were not combined into a single display. Gopher was well-suited to limited bandwidth and slower computers that did not display graphics.

hypertext. A document that includes text, images, and links which are combined into a single computer display by browsers. It is the basis of the World Wide Web.

Hypertext Markup Language (HTML). The language for describing hyper-text documents so that the pieces can be retrieved and combined by the browser.

HyperText Transfer Protocol (HTTP). The communication method used by computers to transfer hypertext documents from one computer (the server or host) to another (the client).

Internet. The Internet is global network of computer networks that connects different kinds of computers so that they can share informa-tion.

Internet Relay Chat (IRC). A method of allowing several people to trans-mit text messages to one another over the Internet. The people who want to chat all link to a particular chat room.

instant messaging (IM). A method of sending a message from one person to another as long as both computers are connected to the Internet and both are running compatible Instant messaging software.

mailbox. Every email address has a mailbox, a space on the hard disk drive of the computer that receives email messages. Email stays in the mailbox until it is retrieved or deleted. Most mailboxes have size limits (for example, 1 or 2 megabytes of email). When the limit is reached, incoming messages are returned to the sender.

mailing list. A mailing list consists of a group of people (subscribers) who wish to exchange email messages on a particular topic. Any message sent by one subscriber to the mailing list is distributed to all of the subscribers.

newsgroup. A newsgroup is a form of electronic bulletin board. USENET newsgroups are grouped into hierarchies that indicate the general topic of the group. For example, the groups that begin with "comp." are concerned with computing issues and the groups beginning with "sci." are concerned with the sciences.

newsreader. A newsreader is a software program that allows you to retrieve and post messages to newsgroups.

plug-ins. Plug-ins are software programs that work within your web browser to handle file types that the browser cannot interpret. For example, plug-ins handle files containing video, sound, and virtual worlds.

portal. A web site that provides access to many features on a single page. A portal usually contains a subject classification of the web and a web search box, as well as news, stock prices, weather, sports, and other information. Most portals can be customized so that you select what features are included.

spam. Spam is the email equivalent of junk mail. It is email that you have solicited and that usually involves some kind of advertising.

start page. The web page that your browser loads when you first start it up. The default page is set by the company that distributes the browser, but you can change it to any other web page. You can also create a simple web page on your computer and use that as the start page.

virus. A computer program that copies itself to other computers. Just like biological viruses, software viruses can be relatively benign or they can destroy data on your computer. They are carried in software pro-grams and document files. Virus protection software is generally effec-tive, but you should still keep current backup copies of all of your important files.

web rings. A group of web sites that provide links to one another so that you can easily jump from one to another.

World Wide Web (www). Much of the information on the Internet is now organized through HTML documents and hyperlinks that allow you to combine text from one site with an image from another site with sound from a third site. This ability to link resources around the world is the World Wide Web.

Universal Resource Locator (URL). An URL is the address of a file on the World Wide Web. It allows the browser to select it out of all the files that are accessible on the web.

usenet. The USEr NETwork is the hierarchical collection of newsgroups including "comp.", "alt.", "sci.", "talk.", and others.